$\cancel{2}5 \sim$

D1601210

German Uniforms of the 20th Century   Volume 1
Uniforms of the Panzer Troops
1917 to the Present

Jörg-M. Hormann

UNIFORMS
OF THE
PANZER TROOPS

1917-TO THE PRESENT

JÖRG M. HORMANN

1469 Morstein Road, West Chester, Pennsylvania 19380

The author is responsible for the contents.

Translated by Dr. Edward Force, Central Connecticut State University

Originally published under the title, "Uniformen der
Panzertruppe" 1917 bis heute, copyright Podzun-Pallas-Verlag
GmbH, Markt 9, 6360 Friedberg/H.3, ©1989, ISBN: 3-7909-0380-9.

Copyright © 1989 by Schiffer Publishing.
Library of Congress Catalog Number: 89-063361.

All rights reserved. No part of this work may be reproduced or used
in any forms or by any means—graphic, electronic or mechanical,
including photocopying or information storage and retrieval
systems—without written permission from the copyright holder.

Printed in the United States of America.
ISBN: 0-88740-214-3

Published by Schiffer Publishing, Ltd.
1469 Morstein Road
West Chester, Pennsylvania 19380
Please write for a free catalog.
This book may be purchased from the publisher.
Please include $2.00 postage.
Try your bookstore first.

Contents

Introduction

In recent years a number of books concerning our military past have appeared. Almost all areas of unit formation and war history have been covered. Scarcely a military theme since World War I has been omitted—with one exception. On uniforms, a very basic theme of military life, there is little literature in German. Several treatments have included the uniforms of the Reichswehr, those of the Wehrmacht and the uniform history of the Bundeswehr. In the USA, Great Britain and France, on the other hand, there is much on the subject. With the series "German Uniforms of the 20th Century", this gap in German literature is now filled.

We begin with the uniforms of the panzer troops. The limitation of one service arm per volume, but covering the time from World War I to the present, is especially fascinating. In this manner, lines of development in the uniforming of one type of unit, or breaks in the tradition, are easy to see. Such relationships are made clear to the reader in this new information on uniforms, with the emphasis on pictorial presentation. Unpublished illustrations of collection pieces and contemporary photographic material with clear references to people and times, are outstanding elements of these books.

I should like to thank the following gentlemen, whose help contributed to the existence of this book: Norbert Kannapin, Jürgen Huss, Gottfried Ingold, Werner Stangenberg and Gerhard Rudloff. I am also indebted to the Streitkräfteamt, Nachwuchsverbund Section.

Garbsen, Summer 1989

Jörg-M. Hormann

A New Troop on the Battlefields of 1917

The appearance of the first British tanks during the Battle of the Somme in September of 1916 really should have had an alarming effect on the German military command. A lack of technical vision and the wrong evaluation of this new weapon led to improvised anti-tank measures by the infantry and artillery. It was thought that the problem could be solved by barrage fire and direct hits from the artillery as well as the infantry's close-combat weapons. The success of these measures in the months before the massed deployment of British tanks made the military leadership look right at first. The fact that this new enemy weapon's vulnerable technology, and unpurposeful tactical use was overlooked, contributed to the success of their own defenses. The leadership never realized that it was possible to bring movement into the unmoving positional warfare with the help of motorized fighting vehicles.

With the Mark IV, of which more than 1000 were produced in Britain, the "tank" appeared on the battlefields of 1917-18 as a new weapon. The first tanks could be stopped only by a direct artillery hit, as has happened here.

It was only after the tank battle at Cambrai in November of 1917 that some rethinking by the military command was needed. With relatively minor losses, the British had gained much ground, this being ascribed to the massive deployment of tanks. Now a project that had already been underway for some time was raised to the highest level of priority. Under the direction of Engineer Vollmer of Section A 7V of the War Ministry, a battle tank was built, which was to go down in the history of war and technology as Sturm-Panzerkampfwagen A 7V, the first German tank. In September of 1917 two Sturm-Panzerkampfwagen units were established, to be followed by six others by the end of the war. Each unit had five tanks at its disposal, of which, it must be noted, only 20 were of the A 7V production series. In addition to them, some 25 captured British tanks were used on the German side.

The crews of the A7V tanks were issued linen coveralls including asbestos fibers as uniform clothing. The hoods were not worn in combat.

A view of the command center of a "Wotan". The non-commissioned officers and men show a cross-section of different cap types, from the "scratcher" to the field cap with and without leather straps.

The armored corpsmen of the earliest days wore leather helmets, which were also used for protection by aviators and drivers. Motorized soldiers of the first unit pose here in front of their truck, no. 560.

The shrapnel mask was supposed to protect the soldier behind the observation slit from the effect of shrapnel from outside. It was either captured or copied from the British, and was scarcely used in combat.

A7V tank 563 "Wotan" with Lieutenant Goldmann as its commander. Sixteen-man crews were the rule for these first German battle tanks. There were as yet no special uniform emblems or symbols for the armored soldiers; they wore the appropriate field uniform.

Free corpsmen before their armored road vehicle in the spring of 1919. They belonged to the "Kokampf" formation (Commander of the Battle Tank Units), which painted the vehicles of their three units with death's-head symbols of the type shown here.

This short outline shows the very limited use of the new weapon, and so it is understandable that there was no particular emblem for the soldiers in the tank units. The uniforms and insignia of the original troop units continued to be used. The one exception was a suit of linen coveralls including asbestos fibers, worn in the tanks during operations. Leather helmets, such as were then worn by aviators and motorcyclists, were also worn during operations.

A significant identifying mark of the later armored troops was already emerging in World War I. At first only the tanks of the 1st Unit were painted with white skulls as of March 1918. By the war's end, all A 7V tanks had death's-heads painted on their fronts, with crossbones added. This traditional emblem, which will be discussed further, was not used on captured tanks.

After the brief use of a few tanks by the Free Corps, the new armored weapon disappeared from the scene on account of the Treaty of Versailles. It ranked among the forbidden weapons, just as did aircraft and submarines.

The First Decoration for Panzer Corpsmen

On the 1921 emblem of remembrance, an A7V tank fights its way across the battlefield under fire. The death's-head symbol was part of the armored troop insignia on the collar panels until 1945.

"In order to keep awake among the German people the memory of the accomplishments of the battle vehicle (tank) units, disbanded in accordance with the peace treaty, the former crews of the German tanks (A 7V vehicles and captured British tanks) will be given a decoration of remembrance, the Battle Tank Emblem." When Dr. Gessler, Defense Minister of the Reich, awarded the "decoration of remembrance for the former crews of German tanks" with these words on July 13, 1921, no one could foresee what role the newborn and now "killed" type of weapon was later to play. But one certainly sensed the significance of this decoration and wanted to keep the memory alive.

In the conferring ceremonies it was further stated: "The decoration can be awarded on request of the officers, non-commissioned officers and men of the former tank troops who, during the year of 1918, participated in at least three combat operations in the field. . . as battle tank crews: the commanders, the gunnery personnel, the machine gunners, the drivers and mechanics in the tanks, the signal and radiomen as well as the messengers in the tanks."

Applications for awarding the decoration of remembrance were to be sent to the Reich Defense Ministry, Inspection of the Motorized Troops. In the process of awarding, a certificate of ownership was issued, by means of which the recipient could order the decoration commercially. At first only the firm of C. E. Juncker in Berlin was given the assignment of producing and distributing the decoration. During the Twenties and Thirties, a number of medal manufacturers produced the decoration. Though only about one hundred decorations were awarded, there were many variations in the materials used and types of production.

The Black Panzer Uniform of 1935

According to the Treaty of Versailles, the Reichsheer of the Weimar Republic was banned from forming tank units. The remaining heavy battle tank units of the war army had been demobilized in Wiesbaden. The memory of the tank troops lived on only in the motorized troops, of which seven motorized units were subordinated to the seven divisions of the Reichsheer. In his authoritative work on "The History of the German Armored Weapon", General Nehring writes: "It is not likely that these new and revised formations were made with a thought of later development of the motorized troops into panzer troops. This conception came into being only toward the end of the Twenties, when the training provided in the operations "Kama" (establishment of a secret tank school near Kazan, Russia) and the gradual restructuring of the motorized units into motorcycle companies and imitation tank companies (with dummy armored scout cars and tanks) became effective. Only several years later would the motorized troops, through their inspectors and commanders as well as on the basis of their own capability, become the nuclei of a

A 1935 panzer company with 25 Type 1 B tanks in formation. For this review the company chief wears a brown belt set (shoulder strap and belt) as well as a white shirt with a black tie.

development still unsuspected at that time."

For the motorized troop units of the Reichsheer, there was special protective clothing, consisting of jacket, trousers, coat and gloves and made of black leather. Also included in their equipment was a black leather helmet, as well as a one-piece protective coverall of field-gray canvaslike material. In 1932 troop testing of a new "motor vehicle protective clothing" began, which led to the introduction in 1934 of the black uniform for the panzer troops and simplified special clothing for motorized troops.

The first "special clothing" for tank service in 1934 lacked the national emblem. The woven or hand-embroidered eagle on the right breast side was to be added only later.

The "armored peaked cap" too bore no national eagle at first. The oak-leaf wreath is embroidered directly on the material and equipped with a metal cockade.

With the Basque beret as the "peaked cap for the motorized battle troops", a new type of headgear was introduced into the German Army. A black beret, with the cap emblem, was drawn over a hard rubber protective helmet. The first oak-leaf embroidery was done directly on the fabric of the cap.

After the introduction of the national eagle, the woven emblem with its background was sewn onto the fabric. The original caps are recognizable by the six vent holes in the form of pierced hard rubber plugs.

Lieutenant Werner, Baron von Beschwitz with his tank crew of Panzer Regiment 3. The photo, with Panzerkampfwagen II, Type F, was taken during or just before the Polish campaign, as can be told by the white cross without a border on the turret side.

From a blend of traditional elements and practical features, there came a uniform that was to characterize the panzer troops through the end of World War II. Pink as the weapon color of the Reichsheer's motorized troops, the death's-head of the A 7V tank units of World War I, and the black color of the uniform were among these elements. The formation of the first three panzer regiments in 1934-35 was done by reorganizing cavalry regiments. For this reason, a connection has often been cited between the tradition of the black uniform color and the traditions of the cavalry, particularly the "Black Hussars". Those who made the plans surely had no objection to this tangent, though the decision in favor of black had more to do with practicality than tradition. Even today, oil stains show up less on black than on field gray or olive drab.

For service with tanks, special clothing of black fabric was introduced for the soldiers of the panzer troops: a protective cap, field jacket and trousers. They had pipings on the collar and its facings in the weapon color, as well as an aluminum death's-head on the facings. The black field trousers had no pipings. The non-commissioned officers' special clothing, unlike other uniforms, had no collar braid. A dark gray shirt and a black necktie were also part of the special uniform.

Colonel Gustav, Baron von Bodenhausen, Commander of Panzer Regiment 31, was awarded the German Cross in gold on April 14, 1942. This photo, taken afterward, shows that the armored peaked cap was still worn until well into the Russian campaign.

The Eagle Emblem of 1934

As ordered on November 11, 1935, the eagle emblem was also to appear on the black special clothing. Since 1934, all German soldiers had worn the eagle on their headgear and on the right breast of their uniform and field jackets. Non-commissioned officers and men wore woven or machine-sewn insignias, the officers hand-sewn insignias. For the special clothing, the eagle was woven on silver-gray cotton on a black background for all ranks. Embroidered insignias were unsanctioned and unpopular here.

A machine-embroidered national eagle was worn on the uniform coat, as can be seen at right above. At right is a hand-embroidered eagle made with metal threads, for the uniform coats and field jackets of officers.

A woven national eagle for the black special clothing . This eagle belongs to an officer's armored uniform that was tailored in 1944. Hand-embroidered eagles on black backgrounds for officers are very uncommon.

The Flag Flies On

The flags and banners of the Wehrmacht were granted to all units on March 16, 1936 by the "Führer and Reich Chancellor in his position of Supreme Commander of the Wehrmacht". In the introductory decree it was said: "Today, on the first anniversary of the rebirth of German military freedom, I confer troop flags upon the Wehrmacht..."

A regimental banner of rose-colored silk, its dimensions 75 x 51 cm. Here the banner of Armored Reconnaissance Unit 3 is on parade in Berlin after the French campaign. The standard-bearer, Master Sergeant Ludwig, has Lieutenant Behrendt and Lieutenant von Viebahn as escort officers.

In the "Reibert", the bible of many generations of soldiers, the significance of the troop flags and banners was expressed in the spirit of the 1937-38 times: "... granted to the troops by the Führer, they are a symbol and reminder of the soldier's sworn oath. They should therefore be sacred to the soldier. Formerly, when the forms of battle were different, the flag was carried on the battlefield. The sight of it inspired the fighting men, made their hearts beat higher. It called to mind the oath that they had once sworn, and the fact that the hour to live up to it had struck. It had gone through everything that the troop had experienced, good and bad days, battle and victory. It encouraged the timid, waved the last greeting to many a dying man. Where it was, there were often death and destruction, but always fame and honor. Thus the flag, in the old army, embodied the history of its troop unit. This glorious tradition is maintained by the flags and banners of today. Even though they are no longer unfurled on the battlefield, their spirit and meaning have not changed. Soldiers come and go, the flag remains and outlasts the generations ..."

The motorized units, including the panzer troops, basically bore a banner measuring 75 by 51 cm, with a pointed cutout (the so-called Hussar cut) extending 25 cm in.

On the rose-colored silk cloth of the banner there is sewn a 50 x 50 cm Iron Cross of silk, its central field embroidered with a stylized

Banner cords made of 4.6-cm aluminum thread ribbons with handworked brushes. The date of March 16, 1936 on the back of the bar indicates the date on which it was awarded to the army. The silvered bars are 4.7 cm wide and 12.5 cm long.

The uniform coat of a master sergeant with the sleeve emblem for flag and banner carriers. The carrying pouch on the banner bandolier, and the lack of an attachment with a carbine hook, suggest a cavalry guard regiment or an armored reconnaissance unit.

Wehrmacht eagle in a wreath of oak leaves. In the four corners, swastikas standing on their points are worked in black with their borders embroidered in aluminum thread (size 6 x 6 cm). The black oak staff to which the banner cloth was attached was crowned by a metal cap in the form of a Wehrmacht eagle. The cap always had to be attached so that the eagle faced forward (always toward the enemy). Flag and banner bearers wore on their right upper sleeve the emblem of two crossed flags in the color of the field sign of their unit, as well as the Wehrmacht eagle and a spray of oak leaves. When serving with the flag or banner, a ring collar of matt-silvered alloy with an antique-silvered flag emblem was put on.

The privilege of carrying the flag belonged then, as now, to a non-commissioned officer with a sword-belt, accompanied by two officers.

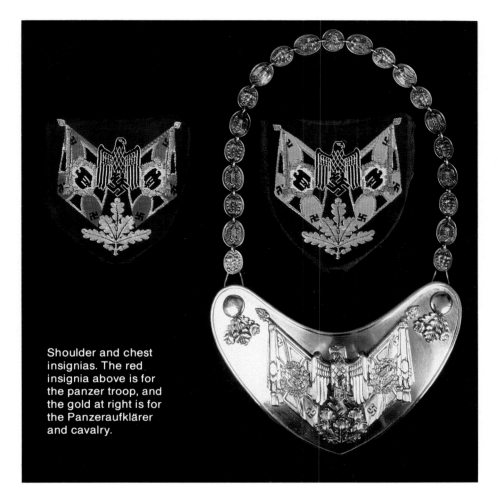

Shoulder and chest insignias. The red insignia above is for the panzer troop, and the gold at right is for the Panzeraufklärer and cavalry.

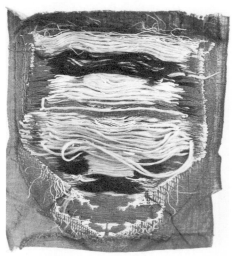

Swearing in young recruits over the regimental banner. The mountings (guiderails) in the banner pole suggest a cavalry regiment. Above: front and rear views of the machine-embroidered sleeve emblem.

The White Coat

"**W**hite coat for officers and Wehrmacht officials of officer's rank," was the official designation for a uniform piece which, according to the rules, should rarely be worn in public. Within the barracks and on the drill fields, as well as when riding horseback outside the barracks, the white coat was a "permitted piece of clothing." In service with the troops, though, the coat could only be worn when the men appeared in coveralls or sport clothes. The first type of white coat,

The "newer specifications" white coat for officers, with turned-down collar but only six buttons. This number of buttons was planned for the "older specifications" coat. The coat with the turned-down collar had eight buttons. This is a general's coat, with golden eagle and buttons.

Major Werner, Baron von Beschwitz in a "newer specifications" white coat, wears the panzer combat emblem with the number of operations.

with a stiff collar, was introduced in the Reichswehr in 1931. A few years later there followed the white coat with turned-down collar and eight buttons, so that a differentiation was now made between the older and newer regulation white coats. The white coats cut like the service coats were made of washable cotton denim with removable insignia, shoulder pieces and buttons. The buttons, as on the mess coat, were inserted through holes and attached on the inside with spring rings,

The "older specifications" white coat, with stiff collar and six buttons. To make the coat washable, all insignia and buttons are removable.

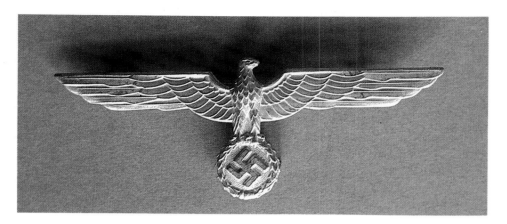

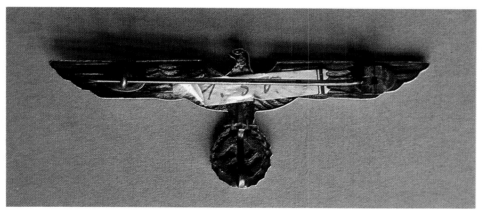

Front and rear views of the aluminum national eagle for the white coat, with the attaching pin. On this piece, the dealer's price tag on the back has survived the years.

which could be removed. The eagle emblem, as can be seen here, had a pin for attachment and was made of silver or gold-colored (generals), hollow pressed aluminum. The shoulder pieces were also removable. Through a slit in the armhole seam, the tongue of the shoulder piece could be inserted at the bottom and held at the top by a shrew button in the hole. According to the regulations, six buttons were provided for the older-type coat, though it was often worn with eight, and with slit side pockets. The newer regulations, on the other hand, called for eight buttons and patch pockets. This white coat could also be worn in public for suitable social occasions.

Insignia of Rank for the Panzer Troops

The illustration on page 29 provides information on the rank classes, enlisted men, non-commissioned officers, officers and generals as well as their insignia of rank.

In 1938 it was stated: "Enlisted men wear shoulder flaps rounded at their upper ends, made of bluish dark green insignia fabric, with pipings on the edges (and the lower ends) in the weapon color, on all their clothing. To distinguish the troop units, schools and command areas, numbers and letters are attached, likewise in the weapon color." For non-commissioned officers the shoulder flaps also had a piped border and emblem of rank, as well as a differentiation symbol, of white metal. During the Reichswehr days, the shoulder flaps were cut square to the field jacket at the top and had no pipings, as the photo of Hans-Jürgen Issbrücker shows. Shoulder flaps of the Twenties were made of field-gray insignia fabric with weapon-color piping.

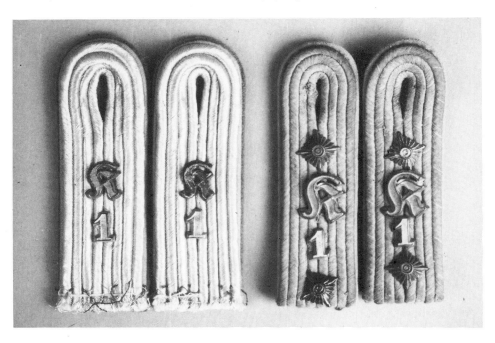

Officers' shoulder pieces for motorized or motorcycle riflemen, with the pink background of the 1st motorcycle rifle battalion. Left: Lieutenant Hans-Jürgen Issbrücker (later Major, awarded the Knight's Cross). Right: Captain Baron von Münchhausen.

As distinguishing letters and numbers, along with the pink weapon color, the following symbols came into use in 1939: Arabic numeral ' armored regiment, Arabic numeral + letter D ' division staff of the panzer division, K ' motorcycle rifle battalion, P ' antitank unit, S ' rifle regiment, just the letters PL ' antitank training unit, S ' panzer troop school, V ' panzer troop test unit. These letters and numbers also appeared in yellow metal on officers' shoulder pieces. The change in weapon color for individual troops is covered in the chapter "From the Tunic to the Field Jacket".

Motorcycle rifleman Hans-Jürgen Issbrücker, 1st Company (button), Motorized Rifle Battalion (K) No. 1 (Arabic numeral) embroidered directly on the shoulder flap, and the double cord with weapon-color panel make his subordination clear.

Right shoulder piece (from the wearer's viewpoint) of Colonel Max, Prince of Waldeck and Pyrmont, as Commander of Antitank Unit 611. Pink background, matt silver braid and gold stars, letters and numbers identify the shoulder pieces for the field jackets of staff officers. As can be seen here, the shoulder pieces are basically sewn into the armhole seam and are held on the shoulder by a grained button of 12-mm diameter.

Below: Shoulder piece of a lieutenant in an antitank unit. The matt-colored flat cords of the officer's shoulder pieces, from lieutenant to captain, on a pink background, bear gilded metal stars and emblems.

Above: Shoulder flap for a sergeant of Antitank Unit 30. The attached border and the metal emblems were silver for non-commissioned officers with and without sword-belt, while here a yellow non-ferrous metal was used for the emblems, as can be determined by polishing.

Above: Left shoulder piece for a lieutenant colonel of Antitank Unit 5. In the case of plaited shoulder pieces (staff officers and generals), the left and right pieces have different button loops. The upper button loop must always come from the back (from the wearer's viewpoint).

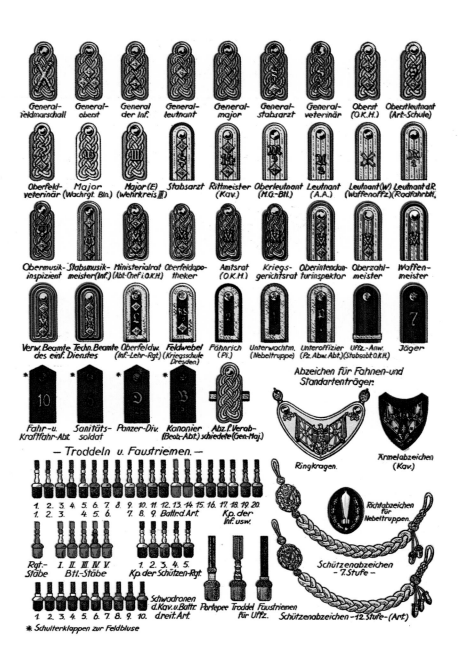

Service rank shoulder insignias, from 1937/38.

Thus the weapon color of the armored scouts was changed from golden yellow via brown to pink, which made the relationship of subordination clear in each case. Several shoulder flaps and pieces of armored scouts with the letter A are shown here. As of 1943, the scouts wore the pink weapon color, as did the other panzer troops.

Shoulder flap for enlisted men of Armored Reconnaissance Unit 8, with raised (embroidered) unit number and weapon-color piping.

Sergeant's shoulder flaps of Albrecht-Friedhelm, Baron zu Eisenbach, later Lieutenant.
Right: Shoulder piece of a captain of armored reconnaissance, with golden yellow background.

The Condor Legion's Panzer Troop Emblem

Very soon after the outbreak of the Spanish Civil War in 1936, Hitler decided to provide help to the Spanish nationalist side. Within the framework of the "Condor Legion", the German volunteer unit in that theater of war, the panzer troops made training personnel and vehicles available in particular. Panzer Unit 88, with its staff, three training companies and a transport column, were under the command of Colonel Ritter von Thoma. The first volunteers came from Panzer Regiment 6 and were joined during the course of the war by men from the oldest regiments of "motorized battle troops". Under the code name "Drohne" (drone), Panzer Unit 88 was to serve as a training troop for the Spanish army in Burgos, to prepare for the future operation of Panzerkampfwagen I and II tanks with Spanish crews.

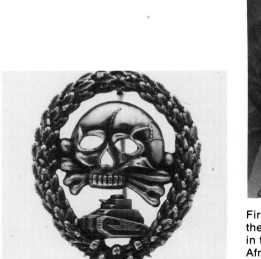

First Sergeant Wilhelm Wendt, wearer of the Knight's Cross (5. Panzer Regiment 5), in the armored uniform of the German Afrika Korps. Beside the Spanish Cross (right breast side) he wears the panzer combat emblem and the panzer troop emblem of the Condor Legion (original at left).

In the very first weeks of their service in Spain, and in remembrance of the motorized unit emblem of 1921, a panzer troop emblem was created and bestowed by Ritter von Thoma throughout the war years. Three-month service in that theater of war and good conduct were the requirements for awarding the medal, which the military command belatedly sanctioned by an order of July 10, 1939.

415 silver and one gold medal were awarded. The golden panzer-troop emblem was given by the members of the "Beekeeper Units" to their commander on the occasion of their final parade in Madrid.

With the disbanding of the Condor Legion on June 8, 1939, the vol-

Panzer troop emblem of the Condor Legion in gold, once awarded to General Ritter von Thoma.

A rare original of the woven armband "1936 Spanien 1939", worn by soldiers of the traditional troop section of the "Beekeeper Units".

unteer members of the unit scattered in all directions. But the memory of the Legion's service was to be kept alive in the form of an armband.

The text of the army's order of June 27, 1939 reads:

1. In remembrance of their participation in the Spanish Civil War, the soldiers of the Panzer Training Regiment and the News Training Unit, as traditional troop sections of the "Beekeeper Units" of the "Condor Legion", wear on their right lower sleeve a 3.2 cm wide madder-red armband with the woven gold inscription:

"1936 Spanien 1939".

2. Manner of wearing: The armbands are to be worn only on the uniform coat, the coats of the parade and dress uniforms, and on the jacket with piping. Location of the armband on the uniform coat 7.5 cm above the cuff, and on the jacket with piping and on the coat 1 cm above the cuff.

3. On transferral to other troop units, the memorial insignia are to be removed.

Saber and Dagger

Side arms were worn by all soldiers until 1945 for walking-out, parades and special occasions. Officers could wear the saber (above) or the officer's dagger (right), according to the situation, rules and uniform. A wide assortment of saber forms was offered by the various manufacturers, with the officer's financial means and tastes setting the standards. In the case of the officer's dagger, the choices were not so extensive. Here the models differed primarily in the color of the handle.

Until the end of World War II, all ranks had the possibility of bearing side arms. Unmounted non-commissioned officers and enlisted men, including all panzer soldiers, were issued bayonets, which they wore particularly with field gray uniforms and on appropriate occasions. Officers could choose between the officer's dagger and the saber. The right to wear them depended on the type of uniform. As a general rule, a brown belt with bayonet or pistol was worn with a combat or dress uniform, an officer's saber on a belt inside the tunic with shoulder strap (until the war began) with a dress uniform on formal occasions and with a watch uniform, an officer's saber on a belt inside the tunic or a full-dress sword belt with a full-dress or report uniform, an officer's dagger or saber with a class A or mess uniform. With the undress uniform either weapon could be worn under the tunic without a belt or sword-belt. The brown officer's belt with a pistol holster and pistol became the standard side arms during the course of the war. Side arms were prescribed for use with the black special clothing as a combat uniform.

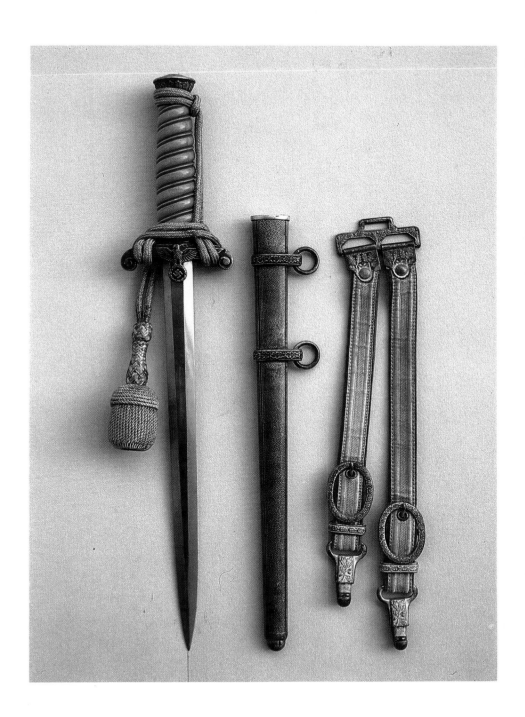

Headgear to 1945

At the end of World War I, a significant change in the appearance and significance of dress and combat headgear took place. The Pickelhaube helmet, shako and chapka, along with the fur caps of the hussars and the metal helmets of the cuirassiers, disappeared when the old army was turned into the Reichsheer. The steel helmet remained, but it was only worn in the field and on certain special occasions (such as parades). The peaked cap exceeded its former significance as a uniform cap, becoming the headgear worn almost all the time. In 1919 it gained the Reichswehr form that was customary until the mid-Thirties, with a black leather peak and lacquered leather strap for all ranks, plus a silvered white metal oak-leaf wreath with a black-white-red metal cockade on its field-gray stripe. In addition, a metal cockade in the state colors was worn on the central

The plate shape of this peaked cap, customarily worn around 1934-35, is easy to see. The crown of this type is round, and only the front is slightly raised. Thus the crown extends out about the same distance over the attaching straps all the way around. The first form of the national eagle for Wehrmacht use is typical of the time. The non-commissioned officer's cord still runs along the upper edge of the collar.

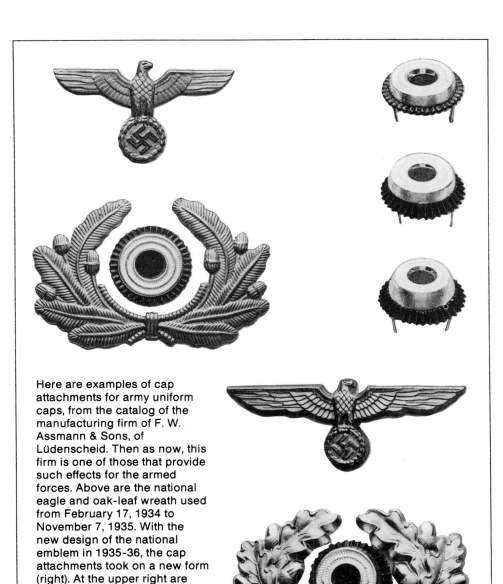

Here are examples of cap attachments for army uniform caps, from the catalog of the manufacturing firm of F. W. Assmann & Sons, of Lüdenscheid. Then as now, this firm is one of those that provide such effects for the armed forces. Above are the national eagle and oak-leaf wreath used from February 17, 1934 to November 7, 1935. With the new design of the national emblem in 1935-36, the cap attachments took on a new form (right). At the upper right are three varying metal cockades. Non-ferrous metals were used to make the early attachments. Hollow stamped sheet aluminum was prescribed as the material for the very high-relief later form.

seam of the cap's sides. In September of 1919 the Imperial cockade was replaced by the black-red-gold eagle cockade. The piping of the peak and the edging stripes were made of cloth in the weapon color, pink or golden yellow for the panzer troops.

With the introduction of silver officers' and gold generals' cap braid in 1927 and the color change of the stripe from field gray to bluish dark green, the development of the army cap was finished for the time being.

In addition to the insignia, only the shape of the cap, influenced by American military styles, changed from a wide, flat plate top panel to more of a saddle shape, with almost vertical sides.

This non-commissioned officer, photographed in October of 1942, has very raised attachments on his peaked cap. Non-commissioned officers with and without sword-belt could wear only metal attachments on their peaked caps.

Hand-embroidered oak-leaf wreath and national emblem were, and still are today, a privilege of officers and generals. The combination of embroidered wreath and stamped national emblem, both silver-colored for officers up to the rank of colonel, is found very often in collections.

Completely embroidered emblems are rarer. Here is the national emblem in hand-embroidered form, for the officer's peaked cap. Toward the end of World War II, production was halted. At right, Major Werner, Baron von Beschwitz, Commander of Heavy Panzer Unit 505, wears a peaked cap with combined emblems.

A peaked cap for an officer of the panzer troops, with hand-embroidered oak-leaf wreath and national emblem plus a metal cockade.

The officers wore as their dress cap a soft field cap very similar in cut to the peaked cap. It had a soft leather peak and woven insignia, no wire stiffening, and no braid.

In March of 1933 the eagle cockade was replaced by the old Imperial type. One year later, on February 19, 1934, the Reichswehr command ordered the eagle symbol of the NSDAP (Nazi Party), varied for this purpose, to be the national symbol of the Reichswehr and later of the Wehrmacht. The new national symbol was applied to the cap in place of the now-abolished state cockades.

The field cap for officers as of 1935 had woven emblems and no cord, as well as a soft leather peak.

Not exactly correctly, this colonel of the panzer troops wears his field cap with a silver cord. Here he is talking to a general of the Serbian allies.

Peaked cap types of the Army

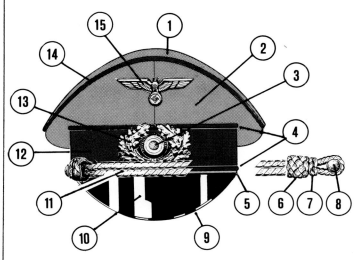

Army peaked cap in saddle shape. Parts: 1. Crown piece. 2. Side piece. 3. Reich cockade. 4. Weapon-color pipings on the attachment stripe. 5. Visible piping of the material. 6. Slide. 7. Knot. 8. Cap button. 9. Rim crimping. 10. Leather or fiber peak. 11. Cap cord. 12. Attachment stripe. 13. Attachment (oak-leaf wreath). 14. Crown piping. 15. National emblem.

Army peaked cap in saddle shape for non-commissioned officers and enlisted men. Recognizable by the metal attachments and leather cap strap with metal slides. The hollow stamped emblems made of aluminum were used from November 7, 1935 to the end of the war.

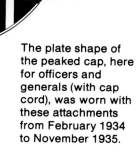

The plate shape of the peaked cap, here for officers and generals (with cap cord), was worn with these attachments from February 1934 to November 1935.

Two versions of the cap insignia can be distinguished clearly: those made of metal and those woven or hand-embroidered on fabric. Hand-embroidered insignia were used more and more often since 1935, and the officers, responsible for their own uniforms, could wear all their insignia in hand-embroidered form. During World War II, as of 1943, the production of hand-embroidered insignia was reduced more and more, and finally ended, on account of raw-material shortages. Once supplies were used up, only metal insignia could be worn.

Woven national emblem and machine-embroidered cockade for the Schiffchen cap.

Field-gray Schiffchen of Lieutenant Leonhard von Heyl, with woven national emblem and hand-embroidered cockade made with metal thread.

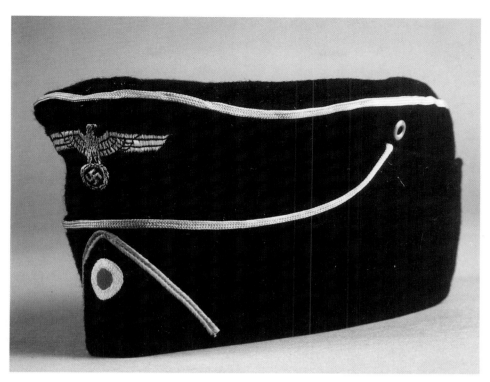

Officer's field cap (Schiffchen) of the panzer troops, worn by Major Rämsch (Armored Regiment 3), with very wide piping on the crown and flap cutout. Woven emblems.

Schiffchen cap (boat shape) for Army officers (1938-1945). Parts: 1. Crown part. 2. Vent hole. 3. Side part. 4. Crown piping. 5. Flap. 6. Inner lining. 7. Woven or embroidered Reich cockade on background. 8. Braided angle in weapon color. 9. Piping on flap cutout. 10. Woven national emblem on background.

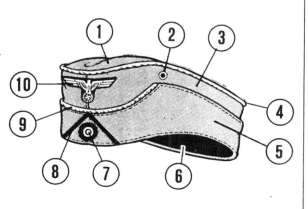

Machine-woven insignia were used most often on soft caps such as the officers' combat cap, the various Schiffchen types and the armored units' peaked caps. The national symbol on the peaked cap corresponded to that of the combat cap, consisting for non-commissioned officers and enlisted men of silver-gray cotton yarn (woven) and for officers of bright aluminum thread. The oak-leaf wreath and cockade were woven of silver gray cotton yarn for all ranks. In the spring of 1941 the production of peaked panzer caps ceased. After that, panzer corpsmen of all ranks wore a black Schiffchen cap.

Lieutenant General Hellmuth von der Chevallerie shortly before being awarded the Knight's Cross in May of 1943, in Russia. Here he wears the field cap with gold braided angle and pipings. The "new test field cap" for officers was introduced in 1938 and offered an alternative to the field cap in peaked form.

Field cap, 1934 model, for non-commissioned officers and enlisted men, with weapon-color braided angle and woven emblems on a dark green background.

Parallel to this, the peaked cap could still be worn. The black combat cap in Schiffchen form was introduced in 1934 as a model for non-commissioned officers and enlisted men, and as the "new experimental combat cap" for officers. The black Schiffchen was worn as of March 1940 until replaced in June of 1943 by the "uniform combat cap". The insignia of the uniform cap were woven of light gray cotton yarn in one piece on a black background and sewn on over the two buttons of the flap.

Here is the most familiar form of the weapon-color braided angle of cotton cord in pink, for non-commissioned officers and enlisted men of the panzer troops. The field cap of field-gray or black cloth was fitted with a weapon-color braided angle only until November of 1942.

The shortage of colored insignia cloth or cotton cord led to a variety of makeshift braided angles on field caps. Here a quilted cord of substitute material has been used. This cap, with hand-embroidered national emblem and metal cockade, was worn by Cavalry Captain Dieter von Puttkamer (Cavalry Regiment 5). The traditional death's-head of the bodyguard hussars could be worn on the cap only by this unit.

Another variant of the braided angle, made of crocheted woolen yarn, on an officer's cap. Golden yellow was worn for a time as the weapon color of the armored reconnaissance units, before it was restricted only to the cavalry as of 1943.

With the uniform field cap 43 for all ranks, the development of army headgear came to an end. This field cap with a large peak, here made of black cloth for panzer soldiers, fulfilled the requests of the troops for a practical cap. The cover, buttoned in the front, could be folded down to give additional protection for the ears.

From the Tunic to the Field Jacket

The Reichsheer had only the dress coat of field-gray fabric with a stiff collar of field-gray edging and a row of eight buttons, patch breast pockets and inset side pockets. Over the years, the class A coat, mess coat and white coat for officers, as well as the moleskin coat, were made to the same pattern. This basic uniform piece changed with the reintroduction of the tunic in June of 1935. From then on, panzer soldiers were issued the tunic and the field jacket, plus their special clothing. Officers could continue to wear the field jacket with pipings in the weapon color on all occasions when the tunic or customary field jacket were allowed. During World War II the tunic was only issued in limited numbers, and the field-gray jacket as well as the black special clothing were issued regularly to the panzer corpsmen.

The armored men's clothing, with the exception of their special

Above: Larisch embroidery for a general on a poppy red collar panel.

Below: Shoulder pieces for a lieutenant general.

Lieutenant General von Brauchitsch in 1934-35. The later commander of the Army was among those who promoted the tank corps.

Lieutenant General Hellmuth von der Chevallerie, Commander of the 13th Panzer Division, here wears the older type Reichsheer coat with eight buttons and poppy red piping down the front.

be worn on the collar of the black special clothing instead of the death's-head emblem, which not all generals of the panzer troops considered necessary. For them, the general's shoulder pieces and the gold national eagle were sufficient identifying marks. The shoulder pieces for generals consisted of a weave of three threads side by side, the two outer ones of golden yellow thread, the

During a drill in his position as Commander of the 273rd Reserve Panzer Division, von der Chevallerie wears his officer's cap (without cord) with embroidered emblems in this photo.

clothes, did not differ basically from the other general issues of the army. Generals did not wear weapon-color pipings, but rather, in place of them, bright red pipings of insignia cloth or gold edgings (on the peaked cap). The identifying mark of the general, the Larisch embroidery on the collar panels, was prescribed for Prussian generals since 1900 and has remained to this day as the sign of a general. Originally the embroidery was done with golden yellow thread around the officer's embroidery (buttonhole edging) of the Larisch Infantry Regiment, disbanded in 1806. The general's patches with embroidery could also

Along with the eight buttons, the inset and swung side pockets are a particular indication of the older Reichswehr coats, which were worn throughout World War II out of loyalty to the old Reichswehr.

Senior General Guderian, creator of the German panzer corps, still wears the Reichswehr era general's coat during a field exercise in 1943.

A group of armored officers at a training discussion. At far left, recognizable by his carmine red trouser trim, is Lieutenant Colonel Harald von Gustedt of the General Staff. The officer in the black panzer uniform at right next to him wears an adjutant's cord and a training emblem behind the flap of his field cap. The photo was taken during field training in 1944.

inner one of bright aluminum thread, as well as insignia of rank made of white metal and a background of highly chromed insignia cloth. A further identifying mark on a general's field-gray uniform was formed by the bright red panels and stripes on the trousers and riding breeches.

The officers of the general staff also wore this trouser trimming, though in a carmine red color. Trouser trim was not worn on the black special clothing. General officers in particular, in a spirit of oneness with the Reichsheer, wore the old tunics with eight buttons and inlet side pockets. Those in the know could recognize an "old boy" of the 100,000-man army and thus a general or officer with the best credentials. Officers could wear the old tunics as mess coats until March 31, 1940 and as dress coats until March 31, 1942. Generals could wear the older type of coat on all occasions, even in place of the tunic.

The field jacket of Senior General Karl Hollidt resembles the prescribed model in cut and fittings. Generals' field jackets had the same collar panels with embroidery, national eagle and buttons as the uniform coat.

The tunic with pink pipings, collar and sleeve panels, was intended mainly as a parade, dress and class A uniform. It consisted of field-gray fabric with collar and sleeve trim of bluish dark green piping. The weapon-color pipings ran from below, from the pocket edgings, to the collar and along the cuffs. Silver-colored, grained and lightly arched buttons of aluminum enhanced the "parade optics" of the tunic, making a complete ensemble. The buttons of non-commissioned officers' and enlisted men's shoulder flaps bore Arabic company numbers. Members of the unit staffs had Roman numerals.

Generals' belts as used before World War II.

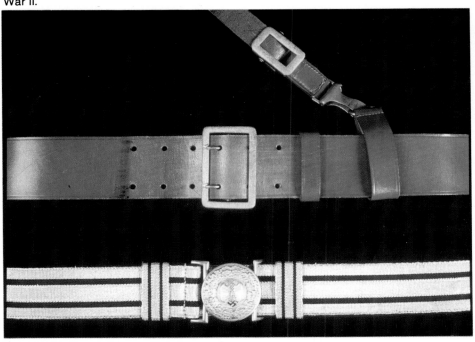

Brown two-tongue belt with gold-colored attachments plus the field belt of Lieutenant General Eugen Hahn (died 1936). The brown shoulder strap was worn by officers and generals until 1939.

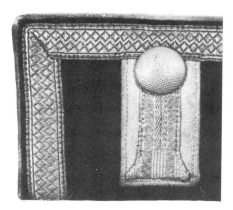

Left: Uniform coat for enlisted men as class A uniform. The handgun with company sword-knot was worn as side arms by enlisted men. A black leather belt with silver-colored buckle was also part of the uniform. On the dark green insignia cloth of the collar and cuffs were the weapon-color facings with cord trim.

Above: Detail of a weapon-color facing with sewn-on silver cord and button plus non-commissioned officer's braid.

Below: Part of a collar with weapon-color piping and facing with woven double cord.

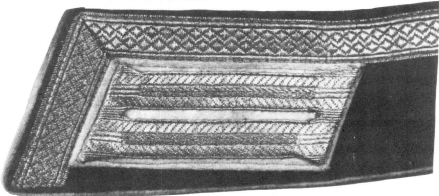

Uniform coat for officers, with shining silver double cords and shoulder pieces. The shoulder band for officers, made of aluminum thread, and for generals, of golden thread, were worn on the parade and special mess uniforms.

The Reichsheer coat of Colonel Gustav, Baron von Bodenhausen, the older type
with eight buttons, as a class A uniform, with weapon-color pipings.

The "field jacket with pipings in the weapon color" of Captain Horst Mämsch, here with an adjutant's emblem as shoulder band.

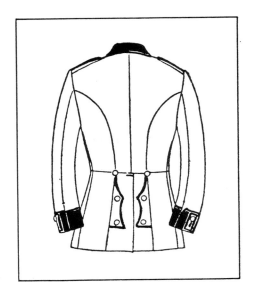

Hand-embroidered double cords on a weapon-color panel for officers, as was worn on the uniform coat and the field jacket with pipings.

Left: Outline drawing of the back of the uniform coat.

For the wedding of their colleague, Lieutenant von Carlowitz, in the autumn of 1940, it went without saying that Lieutenants Hellmann, Rämsch and Stotten (left to right) of Panzer Regiment 3 wore the special mess uniform. Lieutenant Hellmann wears the rare "1936 Spanien 1939" armband.

On many occasions when the tunic was worn in peacetime, the field jacket was used in wartime. The field jacket with pipings differed from the usual field jacket—as the name itself states—by having weapon-color edgings of insignia cloth on the collar, on the lower front and the cuffs. Beyond this, the collar panels with bars, the shoulder pieces, the national emblem and the buttons corresponded to those of the tunic. After removing the pipings and exchanging the special insignia, the field jacket could be worn as a normal one. The field jacket with pipings was, moreover, a perquisite of officers and could

Lieutenant Hans Christoph von Carlowitz of the 3rd Panzer Regiment in his decorated field jacket.

Left: Front and back of the officer's braid with weapon-color panel on dark green insignia cloth, for the field jacket.

not be worn by other ranks, with the exception of an Oberfähnrich.

Officers of the general staff could be recognized by their carmine-red collar facings and a special type of embroidery in cord form, in light aluminum, which was made in bright gold thread on the same facings for officers of the army high command. For the field jacket this embroidery, in matt aluminum or gold, was on collar facings of bluish dark green insignia cloth. The collar panels of officers' field jackets had smooth aluminum embroidery in cord form with weapon-color cord panels on a dark green cloth background.

The field jacket of Cavalry Captain Harald, Baron von Vietinghoff (Cavalry Regiment 12).

Major Bodo-Wilke, Baron von Bodenhausen wore this decorated field jacket of high-quality fabric.

Non-commissioned officers and enlisted men, on the other hand, wore gray woven cords in the same form as tunic cords, though without weapon-color panels. The field jacket was the actual dress coat of non-commissioned officers and enlisted men for almost every occasion, since it was not possible to equip all the troops with tunics during the war. Thus there were many panzer soldiers who were never issued a tunic. The field jacket for enlisted men was made of field-gray fabric with woven national emblem of silver-gray cotton yarn and matt gray grained buttons, plus collar, collar panels and shoulder flaps of dark-green edging cloth. Additional identifying marks included four patch pockets and four inset openings for side hooks.

The officer's field jacket had cuffs as well as matt aluminum emblems (national eagle and shoulder pieces) and matt gray buttons.

According to the rules, no buttons belonged at the place where these General Staff officers had had two buttons sewn on to "improve" the position of the belt. Removable side hooks were used for this purpose on the field jacket for enlisted men, assuring the position of the laden (with bullet pouches etc.) belt.

As the panzer corps grew and troop units were often divided, the pink weapon color changed by the end of the war for some troops. Pink was retained from the beginning by the panzer and antitank units. The armored reconnaissance units were at first distinguished with golden yellow, the color of the cavalry, but

Major Horst, Baron von Uslar-Gleichen, as Commander of Panzer Unit 190, received the Knight's Cross on July 11, 1944. The pink panels of the double bars tend to darken on account of the material, and can thus lead to erroneous identification of weapon colors in individual cases.

Lieutenant Werner Stangenberg (5./Panzer Regiment 4), wearing a field jacket as class A uniform, late in 1943.

The field jacket of Colonel Max, Prince of Waldeck and Pyrmont (Commander, Antitank Unit 611).

The Panzer corps jacket of Lieutenant Colonel von Boxberg (Panzer Regiment 3).

later given their own brown piping to represent an independent service arm. As of 1943, the armored reconnaissance units again wore pink. The riflemen and motorcycle riflemen of the armored divisions at first also wore the pink weapon color, but were changed to green later in the war.

First Lieutenant Werner, Baron von Beschwitz in conversation with a Luftwaffe officer. The weapon-colored piping on the collar of the panzer corps jacket is still present. In the turret is Master Sergeant Alois Klump.

The dark gray shirt and black tie are part of the combat uniform, as worn here by Major Horst Rämsch.

Two photos capturing the atmosphere of the panzer troops and showing some details of their black special clothing. The pictures were taken in 1943-44.

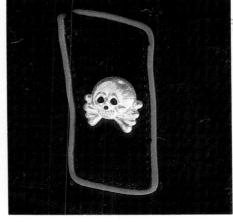

Details of a panzer corps jacket, 1944 version.

Left: right side of the jacket with national eagle and gold-colored shoulder piece emblem of the "Feldherrnhalle".

Above: left shoulder piece with matt silver-colored attachments (two different types on one uniform!).

Upper right: left collar panel with death's-head.

Right: underside of the collar with directly attached death's-heads.

Below: "Feldherrnhalle" armband on the left lower sleeve.

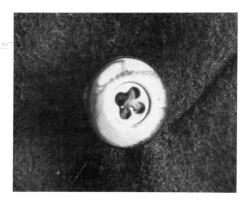

Buttons of this type, made of cast resin and measuring 22 and 14 mm in diameter, were sewn onto the panzer corps jacket in 1944. Cast resin is a substitute material which was used at that time for buttons and similar things. This material is no longer used today.

The most basic part of the armored men's uniform was the black special clothing with pink pipings on the color and around the collar panels. The pipings on the collar were eliminated, beginning in mid-1942. The panzer corps jacket shown in detail here was worn by Lieutenant Werner Stangenberg. He joined the "Feldherrnhalle" panzer troop replacement and training unit on July 26, 1944, and this jacket was issued to him around the beginning of 1945.

Inside view of the panzer corps jacket with the sewn-in lining and the clothing-depot stamp on the right inside pocket.

Werner Stangenberg (Panzer Replacement Unit 4) was promoted to Ensign First Class on July 1, 1943, and to Lieutenant three months later. Within this period the photo was taken, showing the panzer corps jacket without the pink collar piping.

Senior General Heinz Guderian, in his capacity as Inspector General of the Armored Corps, observes a field maneuver from his command tank. The headset with earphones and laryngophone is easy to see.

Uniforms

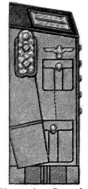
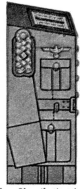

General- Feldmarschall	General der Infanterie usw. (Feldanzug)	Oberst im Generalstab (kl. Gesellschaftsan- zug, Feldbluse mit Vorstößen)	Oberstleutnant im OKW od. OKH (Dienstanzug)

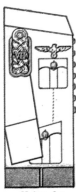

Major der Wehrkreisremonte- Schule VII (weißer Rock)	Hauptmann im Panzer-Rgt. 1 (Feldanzug)	Oberleutnant in der Sturm- geschützabt. 4 (Feldanzug)	Leutnant u. Adjutant im Artillerie-Rgt. 3 Gebirgstruppe (Feldanzug)

In "Oertzen's Pocket Calendar for the Officers of the Army", edited by Count von Westarp, there appeared in the 63rd Edition of 1943 these two schematic drawings of army field uniforms then in use. Of particular interest is the combat uniform for a first lieutenant in Assault Gun Unit 4. The assault guns were subordinate to the artillery, and their soldiers wore the special armored clothing, but in field gray and without death's-head collar panels.

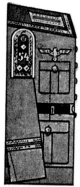
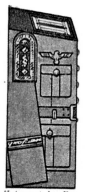
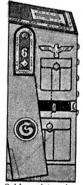
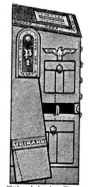

Stabsfeldwebel als
Hauptfeldwebel im
Inf.-Rgt. 54
(Dienstanzug)

Unterarzt im Rgt.
Großdeutschland
(Dienstanzug)

Schirrmeister im
Pionier-Btl. 6
(Dienstanzug)

Fähnrich in Panzer-
Jäger-Abt. 1 mit
Ärmelstreifen „Afrika-
korps" (Dienstanzug)

Waffen-Unteroffizier
in Panzer Division 2
(Feldanzug)

Obergefreiter
(wenig. als 6 Dienst-
jahre) in Panzer-
Nachrichten-Abt. 39
(Feldanzug)

Obergefreiter
(nach 6 Dienstjahren)
und Unterführeran-
wärter im Gebirgs-
Jäger Rgt. 99
(Dienstanzug)

Sanitätssoldat in
Sanitäts-Abt. 5
(Tropenuniform)

A special type of weapon color is found on the special clothing for soldiers of the armored intelligence and armored engineer units. The intelligence men wore the yellow of the intelligence troops, and the engineers wore black and white pipings as collar panels and shoulder-flap edgings as well as collar pipings. The small number of these units explains the rarity of uniforms with these identifying marks.

73

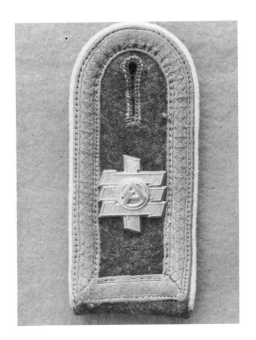

Elite Troops and Their Emblems

Two large units of the army had been given names that were meant to be regarded as particularly significant by the members of all types of troops in these units. Along with the insignia on the uniform, with sleeve stripes and shoulder piece attachments, the "Feldherrnhalle" and "Grossdeutschland" units were given the highest consideration by those in command when it came to weapons and service.

All in all, these units were marked as elite units, with all the accompanying advantages and disadvantages. For the "Feldherrnhalle" units, this meant, as of 1942, frequent reformation after being almost completely wiped out

Runic crosses of the "Feldherrnhalle" with reverse RZM stamp (right) were not the rule for army units.

in the East. Their development had begun with an order of August 9, 1942: "In recognition of the service of the SA in the fight for Greater Germany's future, I bestow on Infantry Regiment 271 the name "Feldherrnhalle". The "Feldherrnhalle" Infantry Regiment wears brown sleeve stripes on the left lower arm with the silver embroidered inscription "Feldherrnhalle". Führer's Headquarters, Adolf Hitler."

On Reichs Party Day in 1936 the "SA Standard Feldherrnhalle" was first presented to the public. This single barracks guard unit of the SA was divided, even before the war, among many of the Luftwaffe's paratrooper regiments and one battalion of IR 271. From these beginnings there developed, by war's end, the FHH Panzer Corps. The soldiers of the FHH units were recruited from army replacements and had nothing to do with the SA. The traditional emblems such as sleeve bands and shoulder-piece attachments, on the other hand, came from SA uniform stores.

Shoulder flaps of an officer's orderly of the "Grossdeutschland" Division, with curved lettering.

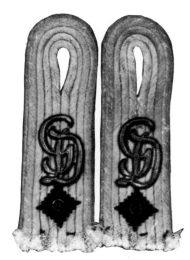

In 1943 the Panzer Grenadier Division "Grossdeutschland" corresponded to the structure of a panzer division. The pink weapon color prevailed in this strongly armored unit.

Above: Shoulder pieces of a first lieutenant, with shoulder-piece attachments of metal.

Left: How the armband was worn.

With the renaming of the Berlin guard regiment as the "Grossdeutschland"
Infantry Regiment in June of 1939, the history of this elite unit of the Army began.
The infantry regiment developed into a panzer corps during the course of the war.
As a strongly armored unit, it belonged to the "Spearhead of the Army", as can be
seen in the service-arm terminology (right). The armband shown here was worn
on the right lower sleeve; this version has the last type of script used before the
war ended. On the 31-mm-wide black strip of cloth, the light gray letters are
machine-embroidered and framed by a sewn-on border above and below. In
contrast to it, the "Feldherrnhalle" armband is woven, as can be seen from the
front and back of it. Here two typical means of preparing German armbands are
seen; woven bands are rarer, and their method of manufacture was used more
often in prewar days.

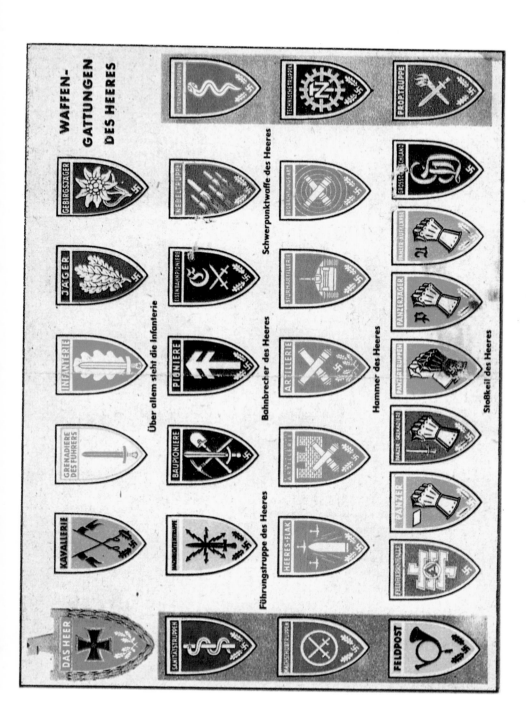

WAFFEN-GATTUNGEN DES HEERES

DAS HEER

KAVALLERIE
GRENADIERE DES FÜHRERS
INFANTERIE
JÄGER
GEBIRGSJÄGER

Über allem steht die Infanterie

NACHRICHTENTRUPPE
BAUPIONIERE
PIONIERE
EISENBAHNPIONIERE
NEBELTRUPPEN

Führungstruppe des Heeres

SANITÄTSTRUPPEN
NACHSCHUBTRUPPEN

HEERES-FLAK
ARTILLERIE
ARTILLERIE
STURMARTILLERIE
BEOBACHTUNGSABT.

Bahnbrecher des Heeres

Schwerpunktwaffe des Heeres

FELDPOST

FELDGENDARMERIE
PANZER
PANZERGRENADIERE
PANZERTRUPPEN
PANZERJÄGER
PANZER-AUFKLÄRER
GROSSDEUTSCHLAND

Hammer des Heeres

Stoßkeil des Heeres

VETERINÄRTRUPPEN
TECHNISCHETRUPPEN
PROPSTRUPPE

77

Weapon-Type Symbols of 1945

"The symbol of the men of the foglayers", says the caption of this drawing. In February of 1945 the Berliner Illustrierte Zeitung acquainted their readers with the new service-arm symbols.

Two large elite units that were supplied with heavy panzer troop units have already been described briefly here. Along with the "Grossdeutschland" and "Feldherrnhalle" units, there were a few more elite units in the army, with special shoulder-piece attachments. Among the grenadiers there were the "Reich Grenadier Regiment Hochund Deutschmeister" and the "Führer Grenadier Division". The soldiers of Cavalry Regiment No. 5 were allowed to wear a special death's-head on their shoulder flaps and pieces.

Such noticeable emblems were meant to make troop units stand out particularly and promote corps spirit. For this purpose, an incalculable number of insignia and symbols appeared during the course of the war and were put to a variety of uses, with official toleration. They fulfilled their purposes just as well as emblems on motor vehicles as on letterheads and presents. Beginning with the regiments, this desire for symbols spread through the divisions to the larger units of the army. Only at the end of the war did these symbols of weapon types begin to cause concern. Until then there were no uniform "decorative arms or emblems" for representative purposes. The symbolic content of these emblems of individual troop types, first made public after the war, was a combination of traditional elements and new creations. The smoke-screen troops and assault artillery used stylized symbols of their weapons, while traditional symbols such as lances for the cavalry, the oak-leaf spray for the mountain troops and the staff of Aesculapius for the doctors, were naturally used too. Some of these symbols are still used as troop-type insignia and beret emblems by the Bundeswehr. But the "iron fist" of the panzer troops has sunk into oblivion.

Günther Stotten, the Typical Brave Panzer Officer

Among the young panzer officers who originally had foreseen a military career with the cavalry was Hans Günther Stotten (born October 10, 1916). In 1934, directly after his schooling at the Real-gymnasium in Hannover, he joined the Dresden Cavalry Regiment, which was reformed into the 5th Panzer Regiment. In the Polish campaign he earned the Iron Cross 2nd and 1st class. In the French campaign the young panzer lieutenant thoroughly realized his potential. His thorough knowledge of the potentialities and his confidence in his weapon, the tank, his personal courage and willing decisiveness brought success in battle. His service in the taking of Chalons was rewarded with the Knight's Cross of the Iron Cross on July 4, 1940. He was the 114th army man to whom the Knight's Cross was awarded since the war began. His further career led him, via the Greek campaign, to Russia, where he was severely wounded before Moscow. After his recovery and orders to serve with the Finnish

On June 10, 1943 Hans Günther Stotten, as Captain and Commander of the 1st Unit of Panzer Regiment 8 in the 15th Panzer Division, was decorated with the oak leaves of the Knight's Cross. A few days later, Hitler personally presented the high honor (second from left is Captain Stotten) to the 236th wearer of the oak leaves.

General Talvela came his service in the German Afrika Korps. Now a captain, he commanded a unit of the 15th Panzer Division and took part in the battle-filled withdrawal of more than 3500 kilometers from Alamein to Tunisia. His reward for numerous proofs of bravery was the German Cross in gold. His capably commanded panzer battle group was able to open a pass. For this courageous deed he was awarded the oak leaves for the Knight's Cross. Being flown out after breaking an arm saved him from being captured by the Americans. General Staff training followed his promotion to major with the Army Group South, where he experienced the withdrawal from Russia across Hungary to Vienna. At left are the medals of honor, campaign insignia, and honors of Major Stotten.

Major Stotten with his mother. At age 26 Stotten was at that time the youngest major in the panzer troops. After General Staff training, he went through the withdrawal from Russia in the Army Group South. On April 4, 1945 he fell in a hail of Russian bullets while trying to escape from captivity.

The panzer battle emblem in silver with the number of operations, 25, which was worn by Major Stotten, as an enlarged example of his medals and decorations, which are shown complete at left. They serve to present a picture of the honored man's bravery and operations.

The Panzer Service Emblem and its Grades

In contrast to the new creation of the infantry and general assault emblems, the armored battle emblem could look back on a certain tradition when it was established. The battle vehicle symbol of World War I and the armored troop emblem of the Condor Legion provided examples for the recognition of armored men's service.

On the part of the panzer troops, the desire for a special armored emblem as an army weapon symbol was expressed to the OKH as early as 1936-37. But only when World War II began did it lead to the creation of an "armored battle vehicle decoration in silver" by the Supreme Commander of the Army, Senior General von Brauchitsch, on December 20, 1939. As of June 1,

Before the assembled troops of Heavy Panzer Unit 505, their commander, Major Werner, Baron von Beschwitz, decorates two soldiers with the armored service emblem. His adjutant holds medals and certificates ready.

1940 the establishment of the "armored battle vehicle decoration in bronze" was added. At the same time, the name was changed to "armored battle decoration".

The army's assault emblems, to which the armored emblem belonged, could be awarded only to soldiers of the army or members of Waffen-SS and police units under army command. Only in exceptional cases (as at Narvik) was awarding to members of the navy and the Luftwaffe possible.

The decoration in silver was awarded to officers, non-commissioned officers and men who, on or after January 1, 1940, served as tank drivers, armored command vehicle drivers, tank gunners or radiomen in at least three operations

On July 21, 1941 the tank gunner Werner Stangenberg (above) was awarded his armored service emblem in silver. The order to award the "Armored Battle Tank Emblem" (left) documents the most important part of the process of awarding.

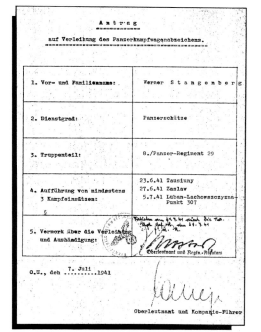

in battle on three different days in which the tank crews took an active part in the battle.

The armored battle decoration in bronze could be awarded, as of June 1, 1940, to soldiers of panzer grenadier regiments and motorcycle rifle battalions in panzer divisions, as well as to members of armored reconnaissance units.

Possession of the battle vehicle decoration of World War I naturally was no substitute for fulfilling the required conditions for the armored

Besitzzeugnis

Dem   Panzerschuetzen

Dienstgrad

Norbert   K a n n a p i n

Vor- und Zuname

6. / Pz. Regiment 6

Truppenteil

wurde das

Panzerkampfabzeichen

— Silber —

verliehen.

Regts.St.Qu., am 18. Januar 1944

Ort und Datum

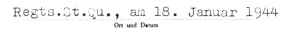

Unterschrift

Oberst und Reginentskommandeur

Dienstgrad und Dienststellung

Oehmigke & Riemschneider, Neuruppin Dr.T. 14002

The decorated soldiers received a certificate as an official award document. In addition, the award was entered in the soldier's record book and military passport. The certificate went to his personal papers. Thousands of armored service emblems were awarded during the war. On account of the large number of awards, a number of manufacturers were given the job of producing the medals, and various forms and materials were used in production. Here, for example, are three emblems awarded to members of the same regiment over the course of time (from left to right, Major Stotten, Major Rämsch, Colonel (BW) Albrecht von Boxberg, all of Panzer Regiment 3). The construction of the medals ranges from massive refined zinc (left), to non-ferrous metal pierced under the tank (center), to hollow stamped non-ferrous sheet metal (right).

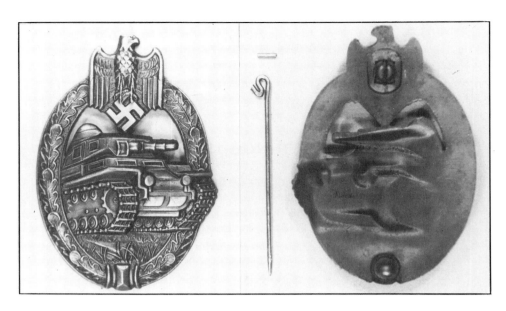

Above: The most frequent type of armored service emblem, here in bronze, was made by a manufacturer with the trade mark A.S. This medal, made of non-ferrous metal, was awarded to Lieutenant Hermann Hormann on May 5, 1941 (1./Motorcycle Rifle Battalion 59).

Below: The armored battle emblem in bronze with operation number 25, awarded to Cavalry Captain Ludwig, Baron von Heyl (Reconnaissance Unit 36).

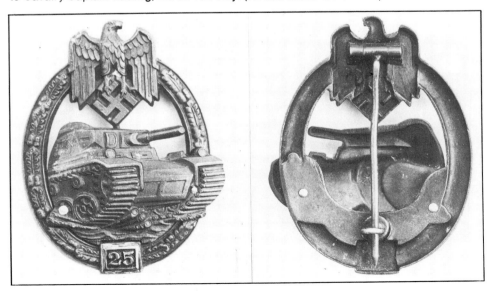

Besitzeugnis

Dem _____ **Obergefreiter** _____
(Dienstgrad)

_____ **Albert Hoffmann** _____
(Vor- und Zuname)

1. Kompanie / Kradschützen Bataillon 55
(Truppenteil)

wurde das

Panzerkampfabzeichen

— Bronze —

verliehen.

O.U. den 1.8.1941
(Ort und Datum)

(Unterschrift)

Generalmajor und Div. — Kdr.
(Dienstgrad und Dienststellung)

An early certificate for an armored service emblem in bronze. The documents usually follow the DIN-A-5 format. Documents in the DIN-A-4 form were given only at the beginning of the era in which the medal was awarded.

87

über die Einführung höherer Stufen zum Panzer=
kampfabzeichen und Sturmabzeichen (allg.)
vom 22. 6. 1943

1. Der Führer hat als Anerkennung der immer erneut bewiesenen Einsatzfreudigkeit der im Panzer angreifenden Angehörigen der schweren Waffen die Einführung höherer Stufen zum Panzerkampfab= zeichen genehmigt.

2. Die höheren Stufen zum Panzerkampfabzeichen werden nach besonderem Muster mit der Zahl 25 in der II. Stufe, der Zahl 50 in der III. Stufe, der Zahl 75 und der Zahl 100 in der IV. Stufe gefertigt.

3. Es kann verliehen werden

nach 25 anrechnungsfähigen Einsätzen
die II. Stufe,
nach 50 anrechnungsfähigen Einsätzen
die III. Stufe,
nach 75 anrechnungsfähigen Einsätzen
die IV. Stufe,

und zwar

das Panzerkampfabzeichen in Silber
an Panzerbesatzungen der Panzereinheiten,

das Panzerkampfabzeichen in Bronze
an Panzerbesatzungen der Panzerspäheinheiten,
das Sturmabzeichen (allg.)
an Angehörige der Sturmgeschützeinheiten, der Sturmpanzereinheiten und Panzerjägereinheiten der Panzerjägerabteilungen (Sf).

Die IV. Stufe kann nach 100 Einsätzen mit der Zahl 100 erneut verliehen werden.

4. Es darf nur ein Sturmabzeichen getragen wer= den; die niedrigen Stufen verbleiben jedoch zur Er= innerung.

5. Die Anrechnungsfähigkeit der Einsatztage ergibt sich aus den Bestimmungen für die Verleihung des Panzerkampfabzeichens und des Sturmabzeichens (allg.); für die Sturmpanzereinheiten und für die Panzerjägereinheiten der Panzerjägerabteilungen (Sf) gelten hierbei die für die Angehörigen der Sturm= geschützbatterien gegebenen Bestimmungen.

6. Der Kp.= usw. Führer legt in einer Liste die Namen der an einem anrechnungs= fähigen Einsatztage beteiligten und bewährten Sol= daten fest, die nach der letzten Eintragung durch Unterschrift des Einheitsführers und Dienststempel abzuschließen ist. Diese Listen sind zu den Beilagen des Kriegstagebuches zu nehmen.

7. Jeder Mann hat im Soldbuch ein Blatt bei sich zu tragen, auf dem der anrechnungs= fähige Einsatztage zu bestätigen und zu beeinigen ist. Für die Führer vom Kp.= usw. Führer an aufwärts sind die Einsatztage durch den nächsthöheren, für den Einsatz zuständigen Vorgesetzten zu bescheinigen; ent=

sprechende Zweitschrift ist bei den Personalpapieren zu führen.

8. a) Die Einsatztage für die höheren Stufen zum Panzerkampfabzeichen und zum Sturmabzeichen (allg.) sind ab 1. 7. 43 anzurechnen; für bereits ver= liehene Infanteriesturmabzeichen, Panzerkampfab= zeichen oder Sturmabzeichen (allg.) werden jedoch drei Einsatztage aus der Zeit vor dem 1. 7. 43 ohne weiteren Nachweis angerechnet.

b) Außerdem können, um den bewährten alten Frontkämpfer hervorzuheben, bei ununterbrochenem Einsatz im Osten oder in Afrika nach dem 22. 6. 41

von 15 Monaten bis zu 25 Einsatztage
„ 12 „ „ „ 15 „
„ 8 „ „ „ 10 „

nach durch gewissenhafte Prüfung des Einheitsführers geführtem Nachweis angerechnet werden. Kom= mando, Verwundung (Erfrierung) oder Urlaub bis zu einem Viertel der vorgesehenen Fristen gilt nicht als Unterbrechung des Einsatzes.

Die Einsatztage sind hierbei auf Antrag des Kp.= usw. Führers durch den Rgt.= usw. Kdr. für die Einheiten usw. festzulegen.

c) Der Div.Kdr. kann an Soldaten, für die durch schwere Verwundung in Zukunft keine Gelegenheit zum anrechnungsfähigen Einsatz mehr gegeben ist, die höheren Stufen zum Panzerkampfabzeichen oder zum Sturmabzeichen (allg.) verleihen.

Hierbei muß der zu Beleihende für den Erwerb
der II. Stufe mindestens 18 Einsatztage
der III. Stufe mindestens 35 Einsatztage
der IV. Stufe mindestens 60 Einsatztage
nachweisen.

Für die Anrechnung von Einsatztagen vor dem 1. 7. 43 siehe vorstehend unter b).

9. An Beliehene werden von den verleihenden Rgts.= usw. Kommandeuren besondere Besitzurkunden nach Muster ausgestellt.

10. Die für die Verleihung von Panzerkampf= abzeichen und Sturmabzeichen (allg.) gegebenen Be= stimmungen gelten auch für die Verleihung der höhe= ren Stufen, soweit im Vorstehenden nicht eine be= sondere Regelung getroffen worden ist.

11. Der monatliche Bedarf an höheren Stufen zum Panzerkampfabzeichen und Sturmabzeichen (allg.) ist von den Heeresgruppen und selbständigen AOK.'s ge= sammelt für sämtliche unterstellten Einheiten bis zum 25. j. M. bei OKH/PA/P 5 (f) anzufordern.

J. A.: Schmundt

OKH., 22. 6. 43 — 13053/43 — PA/P 5 (f)

The codified regulations for the introduction of higher degrees of the armored service emblem give an overview of the conditions for awarding it. In addition, the steps in process of awarding are prescribed here. The process of awarding decorations in the Wehrmacht was very precisely regulated, and the Army had a 295-page instruction book entitled Merkblatt 15/5 "Orders and Emblems of Honor", including all the applicable regulations.

Beſitzeugnis

Dem **Unteroffizier**

(Dienſtgrad)

Rudolf Vogel

(Vor- und Zuname)

2./Panzer-Regiment 36

(Truppenteil)

verleihe ich für tapfere Teilnahme an **28** Einſatztagen

die **II.** Stufe zum

Panzerkampfabzeichen in Silber *)

O.U., 25.5.1944.

(Ort und Datum)   (Unterſchrift)

Major u. Abt.-Kommandeur.

(Dienſtgrad, Dienſtſtellung)

*) bzw. „zum Panzerkampfabzeichen in Bronze" oder „zum Sturmabzeichen (allg.)";
für die erneute Verleihung der IV. Stufe nach 100 Einſatztagen mit dem Zuſatz
„mit der Zahl 100" (nach Stufe).

Beſtell Nr. **1384** Hermann Beyer & Söhne (Beyer & Mann) Langensalza   Din A 5

The form of this certificate allowed a variety of entries. Printed as a model in the General Army Communications, it was obviously regarded as only a model by the supplying printer too. This model was then filled out at the front and turned in.

The armored service emblem in silver for the third level, after 50 days of action, awarded to Major von Beschwitz in December of 1944.

How the armored service emblem was worn, at right next to the Iron Cross First Class and somewhat lower, can be seen clearly in this picture of Major von Beschwitz, and was so prescribed for the assault emblem as well.

battle decoration, and both decorations could be worn simultaneously.

The order for the introduction of higher grades of the armored battle decoration is reproduced here. The silver emblem of the second and third grades portrays a gray tank, while the bronze emblem is thoroughly bronze-colored. The fourth grade includes a golden oak-leaf wreath and a silver or bronze tank.

BESITZZEUGNIS

DEM .... Major
.... (DIENSTGRAD)

........Werner....Frhr..v.B.e.s.c.h.w.i.t.z
.... (VOR- UND FAMILIENNAME)

........s.Panzer-Abteilung ..5o5
.... (TRUPPENTEIL)

VERLEIHE ICH FÜR TAPFERE TEILNAHME

AN ....25... EINSATZTAGEN

DIE ..3... STUFE ZUM
PANZERKAMPFABZEICHEN
IN SILBER

O.U., den 5.Dezember 44
.... (ORT UND DATUM)

J.A.

.... (UNTERSCHRIFT)

Oberst im Oberkommando des Heeres
.... (DIENSTGRAD UND DIENSTSTELLUNG)

(STEMPEL)

In December of 1944 the process of awarding had been simplified, as can be seen from the perfect form of Major von Beschwitz's certificate. In this case, an error turned up at another place. The certificate is filled out for the third level of the armored service emblem for only 25 days, an incorrect number.

The Tank-Destroyer Emblem

In a report on close-range antitank fighting, Lieutenant Colonel Grosan, Commander of the Panzer Training Regiment, told of an incident on the eastern front: "An antitank gun tried to achieve firing position against a standing tank, whereupon other soldiers came and intervened in the action, saying: "You must not shoot, the tank belongs to us, we'll destroy it!"

When the chief gunner disagreed, he was answered by a powerful argument from the field: "Are you going to get a two-week furlough?"

According to another report, a close-range fighter had knocked off seven tanks and been given, believe it or not, 98 days' leave.

For the participants in officer training at the Wünsdorf panzer troop school in November of 1942, these examples showed how motivating extra leave could be. Whether the creation of a special medal for "tank blasters" and individual fighters had the same motivating force is uncertain. The furlough rule, in any case, could not be maintained, and thus the creation

This document of recognition for an "armored close combatant" of Infantry Regiment 430 is not a certificate for the antitank emblem.

The emblems are from 31 to 33 mm high, and the band is 88 mm long. The tank of sheet metal is 43 mm long and 18 mm high, and colored steel gray to black. Right: Original regulations from Merkblatt 15/5 of 1943.

of the "special decoration for the destruction of battle tanks etc. by individual soldiers" also took place.

The conditions for awarding the special decoration were not limited to one particular weapon type, so that all soldiers of the Wehrmacht, with the exception of the navy, could earn the decoration through appropriate accomplishment.

Predestined, as it were, for close-range antitank fighting were the armored soldiers who knew their own vehicles' weak points best, and thus knew the enemy's as well. "Tank fear", that the infantrymen had to be cured of, did not exist among panzer soldiers. Although individual fighting assignments were not among their regular tasks, many members of the tank corps were honored with this special decoration. In 1943 a special decoration on a golden band, to be awarded after the fifth score, was introduced.

Sonderabzeichen

für das Niederkämpfen von Panzerkampfwagen usw. durch Einzelkämpfer

1. Der Führer hat die Einführung eines Sonderabzeichens für das Niederkämpfen von Panzerkampfwagen usw. durch Einzelkämpfer genehmigt.

2. Das Sonderabzeichen wird an Soldaten verliehen, die ab 22. 6. 1941 als Einzelkämpfer mit Nahkampfwaffen oder Nahkampfmitteln (Panzerbüchse, Gewehrgranate, geballte Ladung usw.) einen feindlichen Panzerkampfwagen oder ein sonstiges feindliches gepanzertes Fahrzeug im Nahkampf vernichtet oder außer Gefecht gesetzt haben.

Für jeden vernichteten Panzerkampfwagen wird an den oder die entscheidend beteiligten Einzelkämpfer je ein Sonderabzeichen verliehen.

3. Das Abzeichen besteht aus einem Band aus Aluminiumgespinst von 90 mm Länge und 32 mm Breite mit zwei eingewirkten schwarzen Streifen (3 mm breit), auf dem die aus Blech gestanzte Silhouette eines Panzerkampfwagens in Schwarz angebracht ist.

4. Der Ärmelstreifen wird am rechten Oberärmel der Feldbluse getragen. Bei erneuter Verleihung wird ein weiterer Ärmelstreifen angelegt.

5. Das Sonderabzeichen wird durch den Batl.- usw. Kommandeur auf schriftlichen Vorschlag des Einheitsführers durch Batl.- usw. Befehl verliehen.

6. Tag der Verleihung ist in die Personalpapiere einzutragen. Beglaubigte Abschrift des Batl.- usw. Befehls ist dem Beliehenen auszuhändigen[1]).

7. Die Abzeichen sind über die Division usw. bei den AKK.'s anzufordern[2]).

8. Die Bestimmung über die Verleihung von „Sturmabzeichen" für die Erledigung feindlicher Kampfwagen" behält daneben ihre Gültigkeit.

$$\text{OKH., 9. 3. 42} - \frac{29a}{1900/42} - \text{AHA/Ag/H I •}$$

OKH., 4. 2. 43 — 29e 4 — PA/P 5 (f)

Reserve Lieutenant Colonel Franz Bäke wears the special medal on the armored uniform. The Commander of Panzer Regiment 11 received the swords for the oak leaves of the Knight's Cross on February 21, 1944, the 49th Wehrmacht soldier to receive them. Given the job of organizing the "Feldherrnhalle" Panzer Division in the winter of 1944-45, he commanded this elite unit until the war's end. Below: Retroactive awarding of the medal was possible according to the regulations, and was done, as can be seen here.

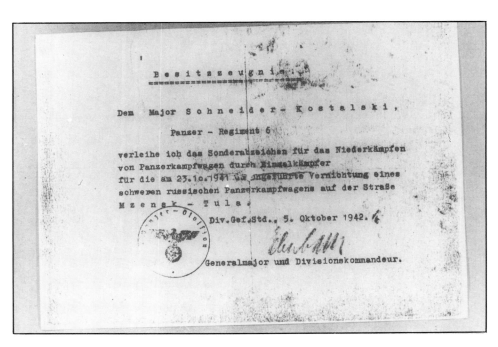

Coats

Though they were very important as a part of a soldier's clothing, the various army coats have been treated rather like stepchildren in the literature. The standard coat used until 1945 consisted of field-gray fabric with a collar of bluish dark green insignia cloth.

Typical identifying marks of the two-row coat were, in addition to the two rows of six grained metal buttons, the buttoned diagonal strap on the back and the shoulder pieces

Two typical coats for officers. Above, Major Horst Rämsch (Panzer Regiment 3) wears the officer's leather coat of fine field-gray leather. At left, Colonel Gustav, Baron von Bodenhausen (Commander, Panzer Regiment 31), wears the field-gray coat with leather shoulders at the front in Russia.

for officers or shoulder flaps for non-commissioned officers and enlisted men, sewn on since 1928. Buttoned shoulder flaps and pieces were used on leather coats. In principle, the coat remained buttoned and could only be worn with two buttons open by generals, to show the red lapel lining. Wearers of the Knight's Cross were also allowed to have two buttons open. Motor vehicle drivers wore a protective coat of field-gray rubberized fabric in rough weather.

Left: Coat for generals, with fur inner facings. Unlike all other officers' coats, which were always to be worn closed, Generals could show their red lapel facings by leaving two buttons unbuttoned. In addition, the general's coat had gilded buttons.

Right: The standard coat for officers had matt silver buttons and a collar of bluish dark green insignia cloth. Older-type coats were also worn with a field-gray cloth collar. Here is the officer's coat of Colonel Gustav, Baron von Bodenhausen, made of particularly fine-quality fabric.

Left: Winter fur coat for officers. Since all officers were responsible for their own clothing, there was room for individuality in equipping within the parameters of the "allowable prescriptions". The field-gray color and the double row of six metal buttons each, plus buttoned shoulder pieces, were required. The national eagle was not worn on the coat.

Right: Winter fur coat for operations at the front. This coat was worn by Major Wendt von Sierakowski (Colonel BW) in Russia. It is cut rather like the army coat but is shorter. On these coats, also known as "bare fur", insignia of rank were worn as planned for camouflage and special clothing.

Above: Lieutenant Ludwig von Heyl (Reconnaissance Unit 36) wearing the protective coat for motor vehicle drivers, made of field-gray rubberized cloth. On his black armored Schiffchen cap, Lieutenant von Heyl wears the "dragoon eagle" as a traditional emblem of Cavalry Regiment 6.

Left: Major Horst Rämsch again in his field-gray leather officer's coat. Here the resemblance to the accepted cut of the cloth coat can be seen clearly.

The Bundeswehr Panzer Troops as of 1956

After the failure of the attempt to set up a European defense community (EVG), the German planners saw that they needed to design an individual uniform for the Bundeswehr. A three-part clothing concept for the army soldiers was conceived, including the slate-gray dress and class A uniform, an olive fatigue suit, and a battle dress in camouflage colors. For tank service an armored combination was developed, which was issued to the troops after the establishment of the first armored units. In transition, the fatigue suit was used for service on and with the armored vehicles. Although the black color of the old

On the occasion of a press conference in 1956, the new uniforms of the Bundeswehr were introduced and presented in this form. All three branches, Army, Air Force and Navy, are seen here with various uniforms and components.

Service arm symbol in old-gold non-ferrous metal for the armored pursuit units, in which the arrows on which the tank is superimposed symbolize the "pursuit assignment".

Armored Reconnaissance Captain Fritz von Schönberg shows how the service-arm emblem for the armored troops is to be worn on the corners of the collar. The sharp point of the shoulder flap is also clear to see.

protective clothing had its advantages and is still worn today by the armored soldiers of various nations, it was no longer retained by the Bundeswehr. Along with the political-historical implications (confusion with the usual SS uniform), modern considerations of the necessity of camouflage also played an important role in the decision for an olive green color. Black is a relatively eye-catching color in the country.

Something new for the armored soldiers was the wearing of troop-type emblems on the collar corners of the fatigue suit and the dress

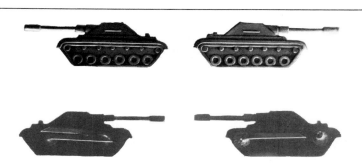

For two service-arm emblems, worn only from November 12, 1955 to December 5, 1956, a special production method was necessary. The armored corps and the medical corps needed two different emblems for the right and left collar corners, with appropriate "aim" of the tank gun and "twist" of the snake on the caduceus. The other emblems had a symmetrical design.

coat. The American origin of these emblems was very clear, and because there was absolutely no tradition of this type of emblem to be seen in the German army, these collar-corner insignia had only a short life. Collar panels with weapon-color backgrounds and Prussian double-cord embroidery came back into use. Rose red remained the distinguishing color of the armored troops, and the armored reconnaissance troops retained their traditional golden yellow. The weapon color appeared on the collar panels at the beginning of the Sixties, as well as on the background of the shoulder flaps for all ranks, and as piping on the gray trousers for everyone but generals. In addition, the peaked caps and gray Schiffchen caps of non-commissioned officers and enlisted men were made with pipings in the service colors.

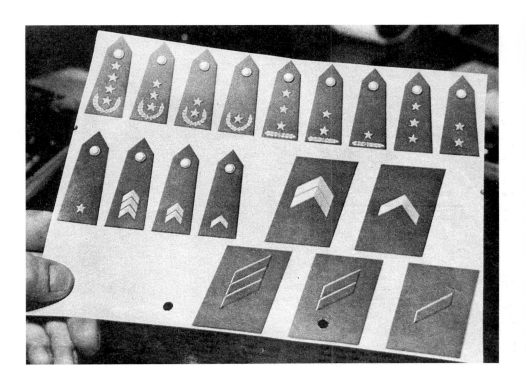

The symbolism of the insignia of rank in the planned European Army of the Fifties showed the Allied influence. The origin of sleeve stripes and chevrons, and of the five-pointed stars, is clearly American. After changing the symbols, the order of rank was kept for the Bundeswehr. Thus the Prussian-German four-pointed star was retained and the straight oak-leaf bar of staff officers lasted only a short time on shoulder flaps.

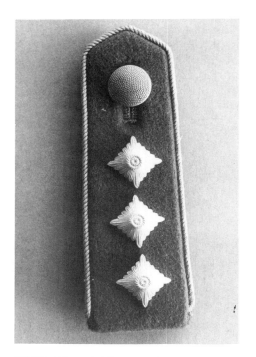

After the old-gold stars of the first few months, chrome stars were worn on the pointed shoulder flaps of officers as of August 1, 1956, as the shoulder flap for a captain's coat (left) shows.

Below: Forerunner of the insignia of rank on the upper sleeve of the armored combination. Worn by Armored Reconnaissance Major F. K. T., Baron von Düsterlohe.

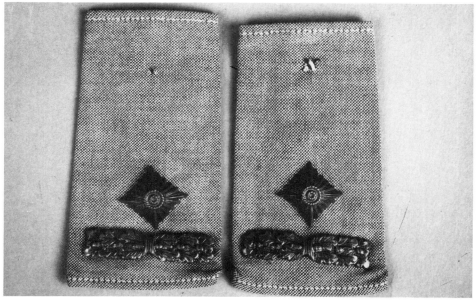

Heer und Luftwaffe
Dienstgradabzeichen
Mannschaften, einfache und gehobene Unteroffiziere

Soldat Gefreiter Obergefreiter Hauptgefreiter

Unteroffizier

Abzeichen auf beiden Ärmeln

Kragenumrandung
bei allen Unteroffizieren altgold

Stabsunteroffizier

Feldwebel Oberfeldwebel Stabsfeldwebel Oberstabsfeldwebel

Aufsteck-
schlaufe
für Fahnen-
junker und
Fähnriche

Heer und Luftwaffe
Dienstgradabzeichen Offiziere

Leutnant	Oberleutnant	Hauptmann

Kragenpaspel chromfarben

Major	Oberstleutnant	Oberst

Brigadegeneral	Generalmajor	Generalleutnant

Kragenpaspel goldfarben

On the rounded shoulder flaps with weapon-color pipings, the old-gold "sergeant's chevron" of the first level were used for many years before being replaced by raised antique silver-colored chevrons.

Below: The introduction of rounded shoulder flaps with weapon-color backgrounds took place in 1962. One can actually speak of shoulder pieces again. Stiffened by a firm inlay, they bore stars of rank and oak leaves of metal or hand embroidery, as the two pairs of shoulder pieces of Armored Corps Colonel Werner, Baron von Beschwitz show.

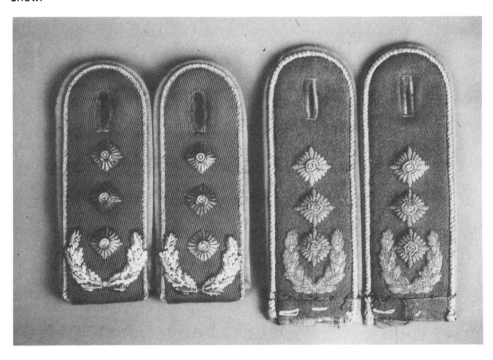

After the establishment of the Bundeswehr there were several additions to the order of ranks, and they brought new insignia of rank with them. In June of 1957, for example, the rank of Hauptfeldwebel (first sergeant) was introduced, and the so-called "head chevron" was introduced as an insignia of rank for the Bundeswehr.

By now all the chevrons and stripes of non-commissioned officers and enlisted men without sword-belts, originally sewn onto the upper sleeves of uniform clothing, have moved to the shoulder flaps and consist of antique silver-colored metal emblems. On the olive fatigues and the battle dress, insignia of rank are worn as pull-on loops over the shoulder flaps. The arm of the service is recognized by a weapon-color cotton band at the lower edge of the loop. Insignia of rank are worn on the upper sleeves of the armored combination outfits.

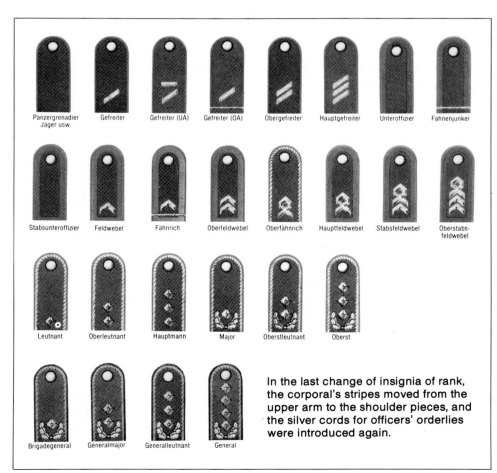

Panzergrenadier Jäger usw.   Gefreiter   Gefreiter (UA)   Gefreiter (OA)   Obergefreiter   Hauptgefreiter   Unteroffizier   Fahnenjunker

Stabsunteroffizier   Feldwebel   Fähnrich   Oberfeldwebel   Oberfähnrich   Hauptfeldwebel   Stabsfeldwebel   Oberstabsfeldwebel

Leutnant   Oberleutnant   Hauptmann   Major   Oberstleutnant   Oberst

Brigadegeneral   Generalmajor   Generalleutnant   General

In the last change of insignia of rank, the corporal's stripes moved from the upper arm to the shoulder pieces, and the silver cords for officers' orderlies were introduced again.

Combinations for Panzer Corpsmen

The black armored clothing had finished its service as a dress and battle uniform by 1945. With the overalls of the American troops in mind, the planners decided in 1956 in favor of an armored combination as protective clothing during tank service. Two models of the tank kombi, as it was known in Bundeswehr slang, can be differentiated. The first type had evenly inset breast pockets. In the new version, used since 1960, these breast pockets were cut diagonally to allow better access from above. The tank kombi, made of weathertight material and with many good qualities, offers the advantage that one can hardly snag it on anything in the tank. All pockets are equipped with zippers. In the back of the

Above: Armored combination and olive peaked cap of 1968. The ridge of the peaked cap under the strap is visible.

Left: Woven insignia of rank were worn on the armored combination, on the upper sleeve below the arm-hole seam. The first versions were relatively small and hard to see on the combinations (old gold).

combination there is an opening from which the rescue line can be drawn. This loop of strong belt material runs down the back to the legs and allows a wounded armored soldier to be pulled out of the tank through the hatches. No shoulder flaps are worn on the combination. Woven insignia of rank of light gray thread on an olive background are sewn onto the upper sleeves. The armored man's weapons include the "Uzi" machine pistol, the 9-mm "P 1" pistol, a variation of the "P 38" Wehrmacht pistol, which can be carried in a buttoned leather holster under the tank combination. As battle headgear, the soldiers of the

An armored pursuit soldier with the 1970 peaked cap.

The wearing of various belts with the armored combination, and the emblems on the peaked caps (metal or woven), are of interest here. From left to right: Colonel Klemmer (Commander, Armored Grenadier Brigade 35), OTL Zobel (new Commander, Armored Battalion 354), and OTL Baron von Beschwitz (former Commander, Armored Battalion 354), at the change of command on August 11, 1968.

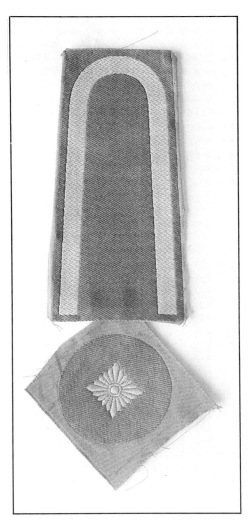

Above: Light gray woven insignia of rank of an officer candidate of 1972. The officer's orderly's star was abolished soon afterward.

Right: A sergeant of today in the new armored combination, with angled breast pockets.

battle tank, pursuit tank or armored reconnaissance units were issued an olive peaked cap, much resembling the black armored peaked cap of 1935. The olive cover with its emblem was pulled on over a leather and plastic peaked cap. This emblem, the national cockade and two crossed sabers, was made of raised metal or woven. With the introduction of the armored beret for the battle tank and armored reconnaissance units in the early Seventies, the olive peaked cap disappeared. The armored pursuit units, though, which belonged to the armored grenadiers, wore the peaked cap some ten years longer, until it was replaced by the beret in those units as well.

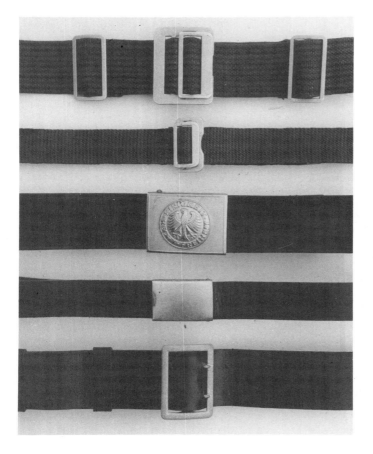

Here is the assortment of leather belts worn by Colonel Baron von Beschwitz during his Bundeswehr service. Belts of American origin, worn with all types of uniform in the earliest Bundeswehr days, were later used only with the dress and combat uniforms and then replaced by the present-day olive belt with box buckle. In 1962 the Bundeswehr reintroduced the traditional leather belt with silvered box buckle and stamped national eagle.

Gray as the Uniform Color

After the first citizens had appeared in uniform, an extensive discussion of the slate-gray color of the new army coat and its details began. The basic color was too dark, the cut of the uniform jacket was too un-military, the insignia of the service arm too American—the list of complaints could have gone on indefinitely. As a result, weapon-color collar panels were introduced at the end of 1956, and a new uniform in the "old" cut a few months later. The gray four-pocket coat now looked like the Wehrmacht's Luftwaffe coat,

The slate-gray coat of a sergeant major of the armored troops, as was still worn in 1962 (when unit emblems were introduced).

After the elimination of service-arm emblems in December of 1956, weapon-color collar panels were introduced.

Dienstanzug

Sommer

Stand: 1.2.1956

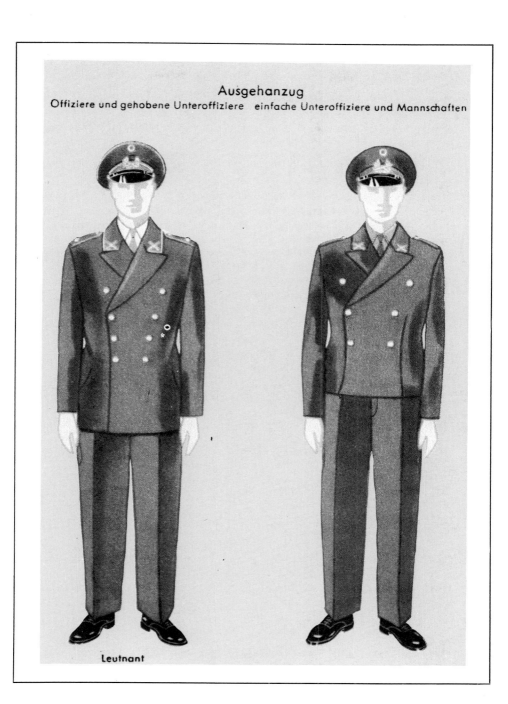

Ausgehanzug
Offiziere und gehobene Unteroffiziere   einfache Unteroffiziere und Mannschaften

Leutnant

The slate-gray dress jacket of Major Bernhard Martini of Armored Reconnaissance Battalion 3. The cut of this short wraparound jacket is very reminiscent of the special clothing jacket of 1935, if one disregards the second row of buttons. The grained buttons are old-gold in color, and the collar panels show the golden yellow as the armored reconnaissance weapon color.

A gray Bundeswehr coat with shoulder cord, as worn on special occasions. This is the dress coat of Colonel Baron von Beschwitz, with pink collar panels and pipings on the shoulder flaps. According to the law concerning titles, orders and signs of honor of July 26, 1957, military decorations may again be worn on the dress uniform in the form of a small decoration clasp.

shoulder flaps more like shoulder pieces. A particular bit of color on the gray uniform appeared on the left upper sleeve as of 1962. Colored emblems indicated the wearer's unit membership, while heraldic elements of a geo-historical nature indicated the home bases of the divisions or units.

Hand-embroidered collar panels as double bars for General Staff officers (left) and for the dress coat with weapon-color background.

and the trousers were dark gray, with pipings in the weapon color. Collar patches with weapon-color facings and silver cord embroidery had a tradition in the German Army and thus were accepted at once by the soldiers without any difficulties. With the introduction of the dress and class A uniform on the "two fabric" principle, or more simply, a gray coat and dark gray trousers, a development began that led to ever-lighter coats and darker trousers. Within the parameters of this development, the shoulder flaps were given a weapon-color background and rounded at the top. An additional reinforcement made the

For non-commissioned officers and enlisted men, the collar panels are woven in light gray and the weapon color, and strengthened on the back.

Above: A first lieutenant of 1966 with Schiffchen cap and the emblem of the 16th Armored Grenadier Brigade. The trousers still have weapon-color piping, which has since been abolished.

Right: A major of the 7th Armored Grenadier Division in the present-day Class A uniform. Dark gray or black trousers are worn with the light to pale gray jacket.

Two generals' caps from early Bundeswehr days. Above is the cap with the projecting top and golden embroidery worn by the first Inspector General of the Bundeswehr, General Adolf Heusinger. The "plate shape" was soon changed to the familiar "saddle shape", as seen on the peaked cap of Lieutenant General von Horn (below). From the beginning, generals had oak-leaf embroidery on their cap peaks. It was introduced for officers in 1962.

Caps and the Armored Corps Beret

The types of cap used by the Bundeswehr differ from those of the Wehrmacht army most of all in the details of their trimmings. Originally the peaked cap, the field cap (cut like the uniform field cap of 1943), and an olive fatigue cap in the same style were introduced. The field and work caps were then given a form like the Schiffchen and called Schiffchen gray and Schiffchen moleskin. Another piece of headgear for the armored corps was the olive armored peaked cap, which was replaced by the black armored beret at the beginning of the Seventies. From then on, soldiers of the armored troops and armored reconnaissance troops wore only the Schiffchen moleskin as a part of their fatigue and field uniforms, plus the armored beret with any uniform. The peaked cap, Schiffchen gray and armored peaked cap were done away with. During a transitional period from

Embroidered emblems are prescribed for the peaked caps of army officers. From lieutenant to captain, they wear no oak-leaf embroidery on the peak, but rather silver edging.

The emblem of the army in metal, as was worn on the peaked caps of non-commissioned officers and enlisted men before the introduction of the beret.

1978 to 1981, all troops in the army were issued the beret as general headgear. The beret emblem of the armored troops was given its national field on the oak-leaf wreath at this time, and the armored reconnaissance men received their own beret emblem. Officers could continue to wear their peaked caps, which, it must be noted, did not include weapon-colored pipings and cords as in the Wehrmacht, but rather silver or gold edgings. Lacquered leather straps and embroidered cap peaks are a novelty in the German Army.

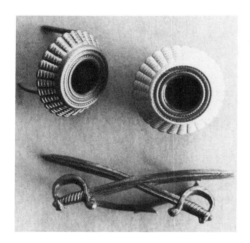

Above: Cockade and crossed sabers for the old combat and armored caps as well as the peaked cap.

Right: At the end of the Sixties a black beret with this emblem, but without a nationality field, was introduced for the armored and armored reconnaissance troops.

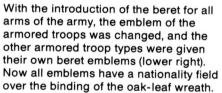

With the introduction of the beret for all arms of the army, the emblem of the armored troops was changed, and the other armored troop types were given their own beret emblems (lower right). Now all emblems have a nationality field over the binding of the oak-leaf wreath.

Peaked cap and Schiffchen for non-commissioned officers and enlisted men of the armored troops, worn as headgear until the introduction of the beret.

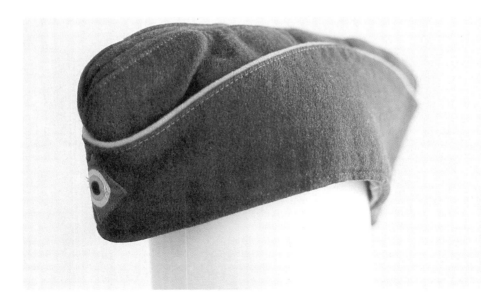

A present-day armored reconnaissance man with black beret and the emblem of the armored reconnaissance troops (armored scout car superimposed on hussar lances). The beret emblem with weapon-color cloth background is not completely according to the regulations.

Present-day Weather Protection

Since the mid-Eighties, a thorough-going change in uniforms has been carried out by the Bundeswehr. The original concept of two basic types of uniform, a field and work uniform (olive) and a dress and mess uniform (gray), is to be changed into a three-part concept by the separation of the work (olive) and fatigue (camouflage) uniforms. Along with this dress reform goes an extensive change and improvement, as well as the new introduction, of uniform

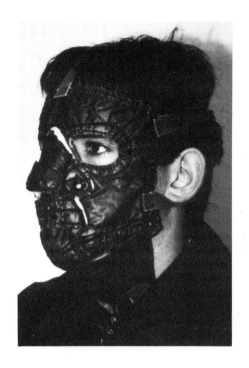

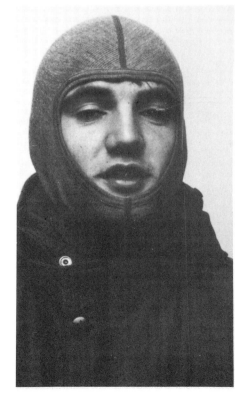

and equipment components. Since the mid-Seventies the combat boots (dice cups) that were very popular among armored soldiers have disappeared—one could even pull one's feet out of them very quickly when the boots got caught in the moving parts of a tank—and been replaced by a high laced type of combat boot. The head and face protectors shown here, and the cold-protector mask, on the other hand, are new parts of the equipment that armored vehicle drivers and crews have lacked since the invention of the tank, for tanks have no windshields.

Achievement Emblem and Marksman's Cord

The emblem for achievements in troop service was introduced for all three branches of the Bundeswehr in 1971, with the three levels of bronze, silver and gold. On January 1, 1973 the final decision in favor of this form of achievement emblem for reservists as well was made. The conditions for receiving this decoration include general military achievements, sporting success, plus specialized achievements and overall aptitude. Included among military achievements along with marching and covering the obstacle course is marksmanship, which is required to earn the marksman's

cord. In 1965 the Bundeswehr reintroduced the marksman's cord for all ranks of non-commissioned officers and enlisted men. The three levels of the marksman's decoration are indicated by the plaquette in bronze, silver or gold on the silver braided cord. The marksman's cord is worn from the right shoulder to the uppermost coat button. To earn the Bundeswehr marksman's cord as in Wehrmacht days—good shooting with one weapon is not sufficient. Today good scores with weapons of two classes are necessary. Like all soldiers in the army, members of the armored and

Marksman's cord in bronze for soldiers of the army and air force.

Machine-embroidered emblem of achievement in silver on olive-colored background, for clothing of the same color.

armored reconnaissance troops can also wear the emblems of their service position and career on their uniforms, in either metal or fabric. For just these two troop arms there is, other than the beret emblem, no particular emblem used today in the Bundeswehr army.

The small clasp of the sport emblem, which may be worn on the uniform.